HUNAN SALTED CHILLI

PUMPKIN CAKES

TOFU NOODLES WITH
VINEGAR DRESSING

JO'S MINI DUMPLINGS

CHIFFON OME

WONTONS, THREE WAYS

Smashed Cucumber

FIERY SICHUAN

MUM'S CHICKEN CONGEE

FONDUE

MICROWAVE

chao ta bee hoon

CHEONG FUN

Yunnan Mashed Potato

SICHUAN PEPPER CHICKEN
WITH FRIED BASIL

ROAST DUCK
NOODLE SOUP

Vegetarian
stock

DONG PO BRAISED PORK

VEGETARIAN WONTONS

STIR-FRIED
SHREDDED
POTATO

WITH

DAN DAN MIAN

Lazy XO Sauce

VEGETABLE
FRIED RICE

soft tofu pudding
with ginger scented syrup

CRISPY PRAWN BALLS WITH PORK STOCK
FERMENTED CHILLI DIP

O-L-I-V-E

A VERY INAUTHENTIC
PRAWN TOAST

V-E-G-E-T-A-B-L-E
F-R-I-E-D   R-I-C-E

Fried Seasonal
Vegetables

PLAIN
CONGEE

BEIJING HOT CHICKEN

MANGO PUDDING

HONG KONG-STYLE
SAGO PUDDING

billionaire fried rice

T0333367

As immigrants with Chinese heritage who both moved to Australia as kids, Rosheen Kaul and Joanna Hu spent their formative years living between (at least) two cultures and wondering how they fitted in. Food was a huge part of this journey: should they cling to the traditional comfort of their parents' varied culinary heritage, attempt to assimilate wholly by learning to love shepherd's pie, or forge a new path where flavour and the freedom to choose trumped authenticity? They chose option three.

Chinese-ish celebrates the confident blending of culture and identity through food – taking what you love and rejecting what doesn't work for you. In these pages, you'll find a bounty of inauthentic Chinese-influenced dishes from Hong Kong to Southeast Asia, including the best rice and noodle dishes, wontons and dumplings, classic and not-so-classic Chinese mains, and even a Sichuan sausage sanga that would proudly sit at any backyard barbie. There are also plenty of tips and shortcuts to help demystify tricky techniques and reassuring advice on unfamiliar ingredients.

This is modern, unconventional, innovative, vibrant, tasty, colourful and incredibly delicious food.

 Rosheen Kaul is head chef at Melbourne's Etta restaurant, where she cooks a menu as culturally diverse as she is. Born in Singapore to parents of mixed Asian heritage (Kashmiri, Peranakan Chinese, Filipino), she grew up between Melbourne, Malaysia, China and Indonesia. To her parents' horror, she pursued a career in food, working at Lee Ho Fook, Smith & Daughters, and Dinner by Heston Blumenthal.

 Joanna Hu is an illustrator and ex front-of-house worker at Vue de Monde, Saint Crispin, and Fat Duck restaurants. The daughter of Chinese Australian parents, she swapped a career in law for a whirlwind few years in hospitality, before settling into a life of painting, knitting, watching crime procedurals, and buying an excess of tweed blazers from charity shops in Melbourne.

To occupy herself during the early weeks of the pandemic, Rosheen began documenting all the inauthentic Asian recipes she loved to eat, and asked her friend Jo to illustrate them. Together they produced *The Isol(Asian) Cookbook*, on which this book is based.

CHINESE-ISH

HOME COOKING
NOT QUITE AUTHENTIC
100% DELICIOUS

Recipes by ROSHEEN KAUL
Illustrations by JOANNA HU

murdoch books
Sydney | London

This book is dedicated to:

ALL THE PARENTS — INCLUDING
OURS, XIAOLING AND BAIDING,
RAJ AND TINA — WHO MADE
THE JOURNEY TO CREATE A
NEW LIFE FOR THEIR CHILDREN,
WHILE CARRYING AN OLD WORLD
ON THE BACK OF THEIR
HOPES AND DREAMS.

CONTENTS

NYONYA PORK
AND CRAB
MEATBALL
SOUP

SEE PAGE 178

On Feeling Chinese-ish

ROSHEEN

If you asked me what my cultural background was a few years ago, you probably would have got a different response each time, depending on the year and my mood. The usual answer was something along the lines of: *'Asian, I guess? Lots of different types of Asian.'*

I fancied myself being Russian for a while, thinking that if I could change my surname to Kaulikova and learn the language, I could run away to Central Asia and blend in with the native population. I certainly didn't look Chinese or Kashmiri, but I could pass for Kazakh pretty easily. I gave learning Russian a go but, admittedly, it was pretty hard. As you can probably tell, identity has always been a contentious issue for me.

I still don't have a tidy explanation or a soundbite that encapsulates all of the diverse ethnicities that make up who I am. There are some that take precedence – those that I am by blood mostly, but some by exposure. Others I find irrelevant, through never having identified with those cultures.

My father is from Kashmir, a disputed region between India and Pakistan. Kashmiris have a fascinating ancestry. They are believed to be one of the 'lost tribes' of Israel, who travelled along the Silk Road and eventually settled in the picturesque Kashmir Valley. Kashmiri culture is an amalgamation of influences from the surrounding geographical areas – Central Asia, Iran, Northwest China and the Indian subcontinent. Here is where the conversation gets confusing for some: Kashmir is a state of India, but I'm not Indian, I'm Kashmiri. Half, anyway.

My mother was born in Singapore to Chinese Filipino parents, but was adopted at a very young age by a Eurasian mother and an Indonesian father. By my count, that's six ethnicities already. My grandmother, my oma, was an incredible cook, predominantly of Nyonya (Peranakan) and Malay dishes. Peranakans are an ethnic group of mixed Chinese and Malay heritage, whose cooking is a blend of the influences and traditions of both those regions. Their food is incredibly unique. My grandfather, my opa, was Indonesian and worked as a sailor and engineer on Dutch ships. As a result, classic Dutch dishes would also make appearances on my mother's table.

My mother's first language was Hokkien – she only began to speak English at primary school. My grandfather was trilingual but because he didn't speak Hokkien, he couldn't communicate with my mother until she started school and learned English. My mum's childhood memories revolve around food – a golden era of visiting local coffee shops and hawker stalls with my oma.

I was born in Singapore in 1992. My mother was native to Singapore and my father had assimilated fairly quickly. We had close family from both my father's and my mother's side living nearby.

We would celebrate Diwali with my Kashmiri family and Lunar New Year with my Chinese Filipino family. In my young mind, both of my parents' cultures melded beautifully and easily together. To be Singaporean simply requires you to identify with the culture – the vast majority of the population is made up of people of Chinese, Malay, Indian and Eurasian descent. While our family wasn't in the ethnic majority, we were still Singaporean. My sister and I spoke with jarring Singlish accents as a testament to that fact, to my parents' horror.

When we were in Singapore, I was too young to be asked the question, *'Where are you from?'*. It was when we moved to Australia when I was a little older that I was confronted with it for the first time. My sister and I were enrolled at a very white, very affluent private school in the inner southeastern suburbs of Melbourne. There were six Asian girls in the whole school – all Chinese and all born in Australia. They were as Australian as any of the other girls, with bags of Tiny Teddy biscuits and Vegemite sandwiches in their lunchboxes.

IF YOU DON'T KNOW ME OR YOU'RE A RIDESHARE DRIVER, I'M PROBABLY STILL GOING TO SAY 'I'M CHINESE-ISH'.

Thankfully, my sister and I were fluent in English (we dropped the Singlish quick-smart) and with Singapore being as advanced as it was, we had already been exposed to the western world, so we had little difficulty fitting in.

It was clear, however, that my sister and I weren't simply Chinese, the most well-known Asian ethnicity in Australia at the time. Our features were more Eurasian, with our large eyes, long eyelashes, and skin tones leaning cooler than warmer. *'Where are you from?'* started being asked more frequently, and I was never able to give a satisfactory answer. Where, indeed?

My sister and I learned Mandarin from a young age in Singapore and continued to study it at a Chinese language school in Melbourne on the weekends. I began leaning on the Chinese cultural traditions I had been exposed to as an easier way to describe my ethnicity. At the time, the Chinese population in Melbourne was only small, made up of predominantly Cantonese immigrants from Hong Kong, with few from China's mainland. Cantonese cuisine was readily available and felt the most familiar, and so we frequently relied on it as our home food. This made it even simpler to emphasise my Chinese heritage when I was asked to describe my cultural background.

As I've grown older, more confident, and prouder of the cultures that make me who I am, I now make it a point to disclose all my major ethnicities. That being said, if you don't know me or you're a rideshare driver, I'm probably still going to say *'I'm Chinese-ish'*.

This is a cookbook filled with all of the Chinese-inspired recipes that have come into our lives: a bounty of Chinese-influenced dishes from Southeast Asia, recipes from Saturday yum cha with family, and comforting food from Hong Kong and China's mainland that I've encountered here in Australia. You'll also find recipes from Shanghai from the time I lived there as a teenager, and recipes from Jo's childhood in Hunan.

These recipes are a snapshot of our journey as young Asian Australians, clinging to (or in Jo's case, flat-out denying) our culture through food, while navigating our way through the western world. This is not a regional Chinese cookbook, nor is it an introduction to Chinese cooking. This is our Chinese-ish story – vibrant, crispy, tasty, colourful and incredibly delicious. These are our tips, tricks and shortcuts born out of late nights working in professional kitchens, but also out of a respect for tradition and for the recipes of our families. This is a book as modern and unconventional as we are.

JO

Chinese-ish is the title we came up with to describe the style of recipes in this book, but it might as well be a description of our identities. I was born in Hunan province in China. A few years later, my parents made the decision to leave their comfortable middle-class lives in their home country and move to Australia – a country they had never even visited, knew few people in, and whose language they hardly spoke. A brave leap of faith that I could not envisage summoning myself.

The Melbourne I grew up in during the early 1990s bears little resemblance to the Melbourne of today. This was a Melbourne where two immigrants could save enough money – while juggling minimum-wage jobs, studying English, completing university degrees and caring for a young child – to buy a house in the suburbs within six years. This was also a Melbourne where I was, at one point, the only non-Anglo-Saxon kid in the entire primary school. This was also the time when Pauline Hanson's One Nation Party and its anti-Asian rhetoric dominated the news cycle.

Growing up between two cultures is a confusing process of reconciling the aspects of each one that you find familiar and comforting with those you want to reject. It was Chinese-ish the way I would speak English to my friends at school, but swap to Mandarin at home. It was Chinese-ish how I would switch between watching my videotape of *The Lion King* until it was worn through, and my videotape of the 1992 CCTV Chinese New Year Gala concert until I could recite it in its entirety.

It was Chinese-ish how, during my phase of only wanting to eat beige foods, my favourites were toasted white bread with butter, and savoury steamed egg custard (蒸水蛋) on rice. Unsurprisingly, it was during this phase I was put on Metamucil in an attempt to up my soluble fibre intake. Parents have such a tough job.

The arrival of grandparents to take care of my younger siblings, who were born some years later, seemed to divide things further. The family home became an intensely Chinese experience: Chinese satellite TV played constantly, Mandarin was the only spoken language to accommodate the elders, and the old Chinese principles of robust discipline (fear, guilt and the underside of an accurately wielded slipper) were enforced. And yet, given the amount of time I was spending conversing in English at school, I could feel it taking over my speech and my thoughts.

There's a way that some immigrant kids inevitably grow apart from their parents due to language barriers. It's sad to look back on the pride I took in pulling further away from my parents, and the feeling of superiority I enjoyed for having an ease with a language I was lucky enough to learn as a toddler that they only learned as adults.

I remember the confusion in the school community over how to classify students like me who were taking Mandarin Chinese as a final high-school subject. We weren't included in the 'Chinese as a First Language' category, of course, as all of our schooling and socialising was in English. But we were usually Mandarin speakers at home, and so it seemed unfair to put us in the 'Chinese as a Second Language' category either. That year saw the creation of a third category for us third-culture kids. How Chinese-ish, to be not quite enough for one side, but too much for the other.

By the time I was a young adult, the number of Asian immigrant kids around me had grown so much that it became even stronger an imperative for me to distance myself from my heritage. It felt like a competition to see who could assimilate the fastest. After all, what if they wouldn't accept us all?

I prided myself on the years when I was the only Asian person in a friendship group. Being told, *'I almost forget you're Asian!'* was seen as a compliment. During those years, the Mandarin slowly seeped out of my body and I didn't even notice except for the occasional phone call with my parents, when the sentences I'd try to form felt foreign and unwieldy on my tongue. Only basic phrases remained, and all the characters I'd learned to read were gone; I was functionally illiterate, with the vocabulary of a 5-year-old.

Ageing has a funny way of showing you the fallacies and traumas of your youth. Some of this trauma might be attributed to the potent political messaging towards Asians in the early 1990s, and some to the silly adolescent desire to erase everything that makes you different. There was an internalised racism that I have only developed the vocabulary to recognise in recent years.

GROWING UP BETWEEN TWO CULTURES IS A CONFUSING PROCESS OF RECONCILING THE ASPECTS OF EACH ONE THAT YOU FIND FAMILIAR AND COMFORTING WITH THOSE YOU WANT TO REJECT.

It may sound trivial, but the release of the film *Crazy Rich Asians* felt like a real watershed moment, when a lot of third-culture kids like myself acknowledged their regret about dismissing their heritage. Perhaps it was the chance to celebrate a piece of pop culture with mainstream appeal that centred on people who looked like us. We weren't all represented in that film, of course, but it was more mainstream representation than we had ever previously received.

I will always be Chinese-ish, that all-important 'ish' representing all the unspoken assimilating and inheriting I've done of both cultures. I've improved my Mandarin language skills in recent years, but I'll never be mistaken for a native speaker in conversation. There's nothing the European continent has done with potatoes that I don't love (although shepherd's pie will always seem exotic to me) but I also think a Sunday roast could be improved with some Lao Gan Ma chilli oil (老干妈). I play mah-jong (麻將) with my grandmother each week, but I will also horrify her by drinking cold water straight from the tap.

Chinese-ish is realising there are no absolutes when it comes to culture and identity. It's about finally finding the way multiple heritages can settle in harmony, unique to each individual and their blend of cultures.

PART ONE

Chinese Cooking 101

KEY INFORMATION FOR SUCCESSFUL CHINESE-ISH COOKING

ON INGREDIENTS

The pantry ingredients in this book can be easily located in the Asian aisle of well-stocked supermarkets and at Asian grocers.

ON UTENSILS

I use a wok for all of my stir-frying. Carbon steel woks are cheap and readily available from Asian kitchenware stores, but require seasoning before they are ready to use. It is also perfectly acceptable to use a frying pan, non-stick wok or a cast-iron skillet for any of these recipes. The instructions remain the same.

ON SUBSTITUTIONS

Most of the recipes that follow can be easily adjusted to suit most dietary requirements, including gluten-free, low-sodium and vegan diets. But if you find yourself needing to make more than three substitutions in a dish, you may find that the end result tastes quite different to what was originally intended.

CHINESE COOKING TECHNIQUES

To successfully cook the recipes in this book, there are some techniques that you will need to have in your repertoire. Some are familiar and found in western cookery, others less so, but all serve a very specific function. I've kept this chapter as brief as possible, but the take-home message is don't be afraid of fire! Learn to love the mist of steam rising from saucepans, the golden shimmer of hot oil and the fiery breath of a blackened wok. Cook with conviction, the way it's meant to be done. Make a mess and deal with it later – your tastebuds will thank you for it.

BAKING 烙
Cooking by dry heat without direct exposure to a flame, often in an oven.

BOILING 煲
Immersing ingredients in boiling water for a prolonged time.

BLANCHING 汆
Immersing ingredients in boiling water for a short time and then submerging them in iced water. Blanching controls the degree of cooking to retain freshness, colour and the original flavour.

BRAISING 烩

A combination of dry and wet cooking. The ingredient is first seared at a high temperature and then transferred into some cooking liquid to simmer for a longer duration.

DEEP-FRYING 炸

Immersing ingredients in oil that has been heated to a high temperature to cook them quickly and, if desired, to give a crispy outer layer.

ROASTING 烤

In Chinese cuisine, the terms 'roasting' and 'baking' both refer to cooking by hot air in an oven.

SHALLOW-FRYING 煎炒

Shallow-frying uses less oil than deep-frying, and is done at a lower temperature than stir-frying. Shallow-fried ingredients are often crispy and golden on the outside, with a soft interior.

STIR-FRYING 炒

Usually done in a wok, stir-frying involves cooking ingredients in hot oil over a high heat, while simultaneously stirring them to ensure even cooking.

STEAMING 蒸

A very gentle cooking technique where ingredients are elevated over boiling water and cooked by the hot water vapour. This method cooks food quickly and retains its flavour.

How to Cook Rice Without a Rice Cooker

Washing and measuring rice was the first task I was given in the kitchen at a very young age. I would rinse the rice three or four times until the water ran clear, then gently shake the saucepan to ensure the rice lay flat and even. I would then measure it using the water line and my finger, exactly as my mother had shown me. In Singapore, we had a rice cooker, and in Australia we have a very useful 'rice' setting on our microwave.

I'm embarrassed to admit that I hadn't successfully cooked rice on the stove until quite recently. With our trusty rice cooker and microwave 'rice' setting, there was no reason for me to ever cook rice on the stove. I was even more taken aback at cooking school, when we were instructed to make a rice pilaf in the oven. In the oven! Some clever soul joked that because I was Asian, I had an unfair advantage, as I had been cooking rice my entire life. They were wrong – my oven rice was a soupy disaster.

To successfully cook rice, you need to follow a ratio by volume, not by weight, and most certainly not by eye. The 'finger' technique is great, but that measurement has to be whispered to you by your ancestors.

White rice can be divided into three major groups: short-grain, medium-grain and long-grain. Depending on what you're cooking and your preference, each serves a different function and gives a different eating experience. The basic rule of thumb is the shorter the rice grain, the stickier it is when cooked. My family predominantly eats jasmine rice, which has a firmer bite and more separated grains than other long-grain varieties. This is likely because we're from Southeast Asia and use forks and spoons, not chopsticks, to eat.

You can use this recipe for jasmine rice and other medium-grain or short-grain (but not sushi) rice varieties. The ratios and cooking techniques will differ for long-grain, brown or wild rices.

PREPARING YOUR RICE

Wash your rice. Seriously. It's dusty and full of starch and grit from processing. Rinse and drain your rice at least three times until the water runs clear. Keep the rice water for your plants – it's really good for them.

ONE STANDARD CUP OF RICE IS GENERALLY PERFECT FOR TWO PEOPLE, SO USE THAT AS YOUR GUIDE.

STOVETOP (ABSORPTION METHOD)
1 cup (185 g) white rice, rinsed
1½ cups (375 ml) water

Combine the rice and water in a large saucepan – I strongly recommend using a non-stick saucepan if you have one. Bring to the boil, uncovered, over medium–high heat, then cover with a lid and reduce to a simmer over low heat. Cook for 12 minutes, then turn the heat off and allow the rice to stand for 10 minutes without lifting the lid.

STEAM
1 cup (185 g) white rice, rinsed
1½ cups (375 ml) water

Fill your steamer with the water and place the dish of rice inside it. Cover and cook the rice for 20–22 minutes over high heat, ensuring there is enough water in the steamer, then turn the heat off and allow the rice to stand, covered, for 10 minutes. Do not remove the lid at this point to peek in or you'll allow the precious steam to escape.

MICROWAVE
1 cup (185 g) white rice, rinsed
2 cups (500 ml) water

Take a deep microwave-safe cooking vessel with a loose-fitting lid and place a tea towel beneath it. The starchy rice water bubbles up fairly high, so to prevent overflow, use a sufficiently deep container. At home, we use a large casserole dish that cooks between 1 and 5 cups of rice perfectly.

For an 1100–1200-watt microwave, cook the rice, uncovered, on high for 10 minutes. You're looking for the water to be almost completely absorbed, with steam holes appearing on the surface. Microwave in one-minute increments until the holes appear. Cover with a tight-fitting lid and allow to stand for 10 minutes before fluffing the rice with a fork.

NOTE
Halving or doubling the quantities will require adjusting the cooking time accordingly.

COMBI OVEN
1 cup (185 g) white rice, rinsed
1 cup (250 ml) water

I know most people don't own a combi (steam) oven, but there are some rather fancy ones on the market nowadays. So on the off-chance that you own one, this is the recipe I use at work for making staff meals, and it's perfect every time.

Set the combi (steam) oven to 100°C (200°F), 100 per cent steam and cook the rice, covered, for 45 minutes. Allow the rice to stand, covered, for 10 minutes, then fluff with a fork.

HOW TO COOK NEARLY EVERY TYPE OF NOODLE AND SOME GREAT WAYS TO EAT THEM

CHAR KWAY TEOW

Smoky, slippery, fatty and rich, these hawker-style noodles are laced with soft clouds of egg. This recipe is for one serve only, because you won't get the same charred flavour from an overcrowded pan. Multiply as required for more servings. If you're short on time, shop-bought sambal oelek is fine to use instead of the chilli paste.

SERVES 1

⅓ cup (80 ml) melted lard (see Notes) or vegetable oil
2 cloves garlic, minced
125 g (4½ oz) fresh thick rice noodles
25 g (1 oz) fresh thick egg noodles
½ Chinese sausage (see Notes), thinly sliced on the diagonal
4 slices fish cake (see Notes)
4 raw prawns (shrimp), peeled and deveined
1 egg, lightly beaten
1 handful bean sprouts, trimmed at both ends
30 g (1 oz) garlic chives, cut into thirds

CHILLI PASTE

5 dried Sichuan chillies (see Notes), soaked in water until soft, then drained
2 fresh red chillies
3 French or Asian shallots
1 teaspoon vegetable oil
Pinch of salt

SAUCE

1½ teaspoons dark soy sauce
½ teaspoon kecap manis (sweet soy sauce)
1 teaspoon fish sauce
1 tablespoon light soy sauce

To make the chilli paste, blitz all of the ingredients together in a food processor to form a fine paste and set aside. You will need 1 tablespoon of this chilli paste (or sambal oelek, if using) for each portion of noodles. Store the remaining chilli paste in an airtight container in the fridge for up to a week.

To make the sauce, whisk all of the ingredients together in a small bowl and set aside.

Heat the lard or oil in a wok or frying pan over high heat until smoking. Add the garlic and fry until fragrant, 10–15 seconds, then add the rice noodles and egg noodles. Stir-fry over high heat for around 30 seconds, then add the Chinese sausage, fish cake and prawns. Continue to stir-fry over high heat until the sausage fat begins to render and the noodles are lightly charred, 2–3 minutes.

Add the sauce and 1 tablespoon of the chilli paste or sambal oelek (use more if you want more heat) and toss to coat.

Push the noodles to the side of the pan and add the beaten egg, bean sprouts and garlic chives. Fry for 30–40 seconds over high heat, until the chives begin to wilt.

Mix everything together, then transfer to a plate and serve immediately.

NOTES

Lard is a flavoursome fat used in traditional Chinese cooking. You can buy it at most supermarkets and butchers. You could also use the fatty top layer that forms when making stock (see pages 51–53). Chinese sausage and fish cake are found in the fridge section of well-stocked Asian grocers. Dried Sichuan chillies are long, red, intensely-flavoured chillies, and they are available at most Asian grocers. If you can't find them, use any other dried chillies.

ROAST DUCK NOODLE SOUP

IN HONG KONG, GLISTENING ROAST MEATS CAN BE SEEN HANGING IN SHOP WINDOWS THROUGHOUT THE CITY: WHOLE DUCKS AND GEESE WITH CRISP AND BURNISHED SKIN, SILKY AND TENDER SOY-MARINATED CHICKENS, AND CRISPY, CRACKLED ROAST PORK BELLY, ACHIEVABLE ONLY AFTER YEARS OF TRAINING BY A CANTONESE CHEF WHO SPECIALISES IN ROAST MEAT. I ONCE ATTEMPTED TO GET INTO A CANTONESE KITCHEN TO LEARN FROM A MASTER, BUT MY COMPLETE LACK OF SPOKEN CANTONESE AND MY ABYSMALLY POOR SPOKEN MANDARIN SHOT THAT IDEA IN THE FOOT.

WHEN I WAS LAST IN HONG KONG, I WAS LUCKY ENOUGH TO SNAG A TABLE AT THE REVERED MICHELIN-STARRED YAT LOK ROAST GOOSE RESTAURANT. IN ROAST MEAT ESTABLISHMENTS SUCH AS THESE, YOU CAN ORDER YOUR MEATS TO SHARE, OR AS AN INDIVIDUAL SERVING ON RICE, DRY NOODLES, OR IN A SOUP. I ORDERED THE NOODLE SOUP: THICK RICE NOODLES SWIMMING IN A BREATHTAKING DUCK BONE BROTH WITH A MELT-IN-THE-MOUTH SLAB OF ROAST GOOSE MEAT GLISTENING ON TOP. IT WAS SO GOOD, I NEARLY CRIED.

LUCKILY, IN AUSTRALIA, OUR CANTONESE COMMUNITY HAS BEEN CONTINUING THIS MAGNIFICENT TRADITION. ROAST DUCK IS A LITTLE EASIER TO FIND THAN ROAST GOOSE, AND THE CONCEPT IS THE SAME: BUY YOURSELF A WHOLE CRISPY ROAST DUCK FROM YOUR LOCAL CANTONESE RESTAURANT, STRIP THE MEAT, AND USE THE CARCASS AND BONES TO MAKE A LUSCIOUS, SILKY BONE BROTH.

SERVES 4

¼ cup (60 ml) sesame oil
6 cm (2½ inch) piece ginger, skin on,
    thickly sliced
4 spring onions (scallions), sliced
    into thirds
Bones, scraps and carcass from
    1 Cantonese roast duck,
    meat reserved for assembly
1 cup (250 ml) Shaoxing wine
3 litres (12 cups) stock (see page 51),
    or use a good-quality
    store-bought stock
Salt, to taste

TO ASSEMBLE

Sliced Cantonese roast duck meat
400 g (14 oz) fresh thick rice noodles,
    or 250 g (9 oz) dried rice noodles,
    soaked in cold water until soft and
    then drained
Thinly sliced spring onion (scallion)

Heat the sesame oil in a deep heavy-based saucepan or stockpot. Add the ginger and spring onion and stir-fry until golden, then add the duck bones, scraps and carcass. Fry slowly over medium heat, rendering out any fat from the duck trimmings. Add the Shaoxing wine and slowly bring to the boil.

Add the stock and bring to the boil again, uncovered, and maintain at a rolling boil for 2–3 hours. Keep an eye on the pan and replenish with water whenever needed, to ensure it doesn't boil dry. After 3 hours, the leftover collagen and rendered fat should have emulsified into the liquid, leaving you with a delicious milky broth. Strain into another saucepan using a fine strainer and bring back up to a simmer. Season with salt.

To assemble, bring a saucepan of water to the boil. Meanwhile, crisp the duck meat under the grill (broiler). Blanch the noodles for 1–2 minutes in the boiling water, then strain and divide between four bowls. Ladle the hot broth over the noodles and arrange the crispy duck meat over the top. Sprinkle with the sliced spring onion and serve.

ROAST DUCK
NOODLE SOUP
SEE PAGE 30

BRÄISĖD SËÄFOOD VĖRMICĖLLI

These lovely saucy noodles are commonly found in Singaporean homes and hawker centres. They're easy to prepare, and you can use any ingredients you have in your fridge. This version uses mixed seafood and some leafy green vegetables, offering lots of different colours and textures. Make sure you throw some stalks in there for crunch.

SERVES 4

¼ cup (60 ml) sesame oil,
    plus extra to serve
2 tablespoons minced garlic
250 g (9 oz) dried rice vermicelli,
    soaked in cold water for 30 minutes
    and then drained
5 cups (1.25 litres) stock (see page 51),
    or use a good-quality
    store-bought stock
2 tablespoons dark soy sauce
2 tablespoons light soy sauce
8 raw prawns (shrimp)
1 calamari, cut into bite-size pieces
250 g (9 oz) pippies (clams),
    soaked in cold water for 1 hour
    to remove sand
2 bunches choy sum, cut into
    3–4 cm (1¼–1½ inch) lengths
4 spring onions (scallions),
    green part only, cut into
    3–4 cm (1¼–1½ inch) lengths
4 eggs, lightly beaten
2 tablespoons Shaoxing wine
2 teaspoons ground white pepper,
    plus extra to serve
Salt and caster (superfine) sugar,
    to taste
2 tablespoons cornflour (cornstarch)
    blended with 3 teaspoons water

Heat half the sesame oil in a wok or frying pan over medium heat. Add half the garlic and fry until fragrant. Add the vermicelli and fry until the water evaporates, 3–4 minutes. Transfer to a plate and set aside.

Add the remaining sesame oil to the pan and fry the remaining garlic. Add the stock and soy sauces and bring to the boil. Return the vermicelli to the pan and arrange the seafood and vegetables over the top. Cover and simmer over medium–high heat for 5 minutes.

Remove the lid and gently stir the seafood and vegetables through the noodles and sauce, trying not to break the fragile noodles. Pour the beaten egg around the outside of the noodles and cover again for 1–2 minutes to cook the egg.

Remove the lid and add the Shaoxing wine, white pepper, salt and sugar. Bring to the boil briefly, then add the cornflour slurry. Reduce the heat and simmer until the sauce thickens, 8–10 minutes.

Serve the noodles with extra white pepper and a few extra drops of sesame oil.

chao ta bee hoon
(CRISPY RICE VERMICELLI PANCAKE)

Chao ta bee hoon (燒焦米粉) is a rare and special dish found at a handful of *zi char* stalls in Singapore. *Zi char* is Hokkien for 'cook and fry' and these establishments offer a huge range of seafood, noodle, rice and vegetable dishes. Eating *chao ta bee hoon* is a delightfully textural experience where you crack open the crispy crust to find silky, flavourful pockets of rice vermicelli. This recipe is very simple and requires little more than a few pantry staples, but does need some confidence with high-heat cooking.

SERVES 4

½ cup (125 ml) vegetable oil
3 cloves garlic, minced
3 eggs
400 g (14 oz) dried rice vermicelli, soaked in cold water for 30 minutes and then drained
1 tablespoon oyster sauce
1 tablespoon dark soy sauce
½ teaspoon fish sauce
1 teaspoon ground white pepper
Pinch of salt
Sambal oelek, to serve

Heat half the oil in a wok or non-stick frying pan over high heat. Add the minced garlic and stir-fry until fragrant, then add the eggs. Fry the eggs, beating with a spatula until they begin to foam, then add the softened rice vermicelli.

Fry over medium–high heat, tossing continuously to disperse the egg through the noodles. Add the oyster, dark soy and fish sauces, white pepper and salt. Stir-fry over high heat until the noodles begin to dry out. Check the seasoning and transfer to a plate. Allow to cool.

Heat the remaining oil in the cleaned wok or non-stick frying pan over high heat until smoking. Add the stir-fried noodles and pat down into a pancake shape, continuously moving the pan but no longer stirring the noodles. This is to ensure even browning. Continue to press the noodle pancake against the base of the wok or pan with your spatula.

Once the bottom has crisped up, and if you're daring enough, flip the pancake over to brown the other side. If you'd rather play it safe, transfer the pancake to a plate and slide it back into the pan, crisp-side up. Fry the other side for a further 3–4 minutes.

Serve the rice vermicelli pancake with a good spoonful of sambal oelek, and eat either by itself or as part of a larger banquet.

DAN DAN MIAN

This is one of the recipes I'm proudest of. My sister and I spent years trying to find a version of *dan dan mian* (担担面) that resembled the one from our childhood. It was always too saucy and meaty, and too similar to another Chinese noodle dish called *zhajiangmian*. For me, the perfect *dan dan mian* is a small bowl of sesame paste-slicked noodles with a sprinkling of crispy pork. Fragrant with Sichuan pepper, dried chillies and *ya cai* (Sichuan pickled vegetable), the noodles are slurpy-crispy-spicy perfection. Sesame paste has a habit of becoming claggy, so hot stock is added, sparingly, to loosen the sauce. Making this in small portions is absolutely essential to maintaining the perfect texture, but no one said you can't have more than one bowl.

SERVES 4

250 g (9 oz) pork mince (ground pork)
½ teaspoon light soy sauce
½ teaspoon ground white pepper
½ teaspoon salt
2 tablespoons vegetable oil
½ teaspoon grated ginger
½ teaspoon grated garlic
¼ cup *ya cai (see Notes)*
1 teaspoon Sichuan or regular chilli
  powder *(see Notes)*
1 teaspoon dark soy sauce
250 g (9 oz) dried thin wheat noodles
2 cups (500 ml) hot stock (see page 51),
  or use a good-quality store-bought
  stock, plus extra to serve
1 teaspoon ground Sichuan
  peppercorns, to serve

SAUCE

1 tablespoon white tahini
1 tablespoon light soy sauce
1 teaspoon Chinkiang black vinegar
1 tablespoon grated garlic
1 teaspoon sesame oil
1 tablespoon chilli oil (see page 94,
  or use Lao Gan Ma chilli oil)
1 teaspoon caster (superfine) sugar

Combine the pork, light soy sauce, white pepper and salt and allow to stand for 30 minutes to marinate.

Heat the oil in a wok or frying pan over medium heat. Add the ginger and garlic and fry until fragrant. Add the marinated pork mince and fry until crisp, 10–12 minutes.

Add the *ya cai*, chilli powder and dark soy sauce. Fry gently for 1–2 minutes, then turn the heat off but leave the wok on the stove for now.

Cook the noodles in a saucepan of boiling water according to the packet instructions, then drain.

Mix all of the ingredients for the sauce together to combine and divide between four bowls. Stir ½ cup (125 ml) of hot stock into each portion to create a loose, creamy sauce.

Divide the noodles between the four bowls, top with the crispy pork and ground Sichuan peppercorns. Add another tablespoon of hot stock and stir thoroughly before eating.

NOTES
You can find *ya cai* (Sichuan pickled vegetable) and Sichuan chilli powder at most Asian grocers.

担担

DAN DAN
POLE

SICHUAN-STYLE COLD NOODLES

I MAKE THESE NOODLES AT WORK AS A RAPID-FIRE STAFF MEAL WHEN I'M PARTICULARLY BUSY. SO SIMPLY THROWN TOGETHER USING PANTRY STAPLES AND SOME FRESH VEGETABLES, THIS SALAD-ESQUE COLD NOODLE DISH IS A WARM-WEATHER FAVOURITE. IN CHINESE CUISINE, RAW DISHES ARE OFTEN SEASONED WITH OIL THAT HAS BEEN HEATED TO A VERY HIGH TEMPERATURE AND THEN COOLED, IMPARTING A 'COOKED' FLAVOUR TO WHAT WOULD OTHERWISE BE A BRIGHT AND FRESH DISH. THESE NOODLES REQUIRE MAKING A QUICK AND EASY CHILLI OIL THAT OFFERS MUCH MORE DEPTH OF FLAVOUR THAN AN UNCOOKED OIL DRESSING.

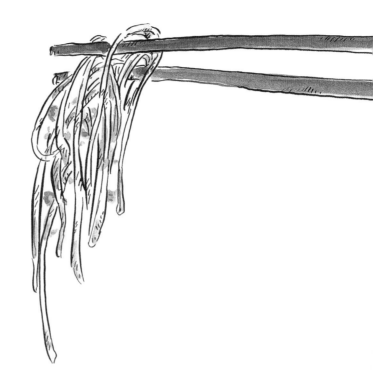

SERVES 4

400 g (14 oz) fresh thin wheat noodles
  or 250 g (9 oz) dried thin wheat
  noodles
Iced water
1 tablespoon sesame oil
2 teaspoons sesame seeds
1 Lebanese (short) cucumber,
  julienned
2–3 spring onions (scallions),
  thinly sliced

CHILLI OIL

2 tablespoons Sichuan or regular
  chilli powder *(see Notes on page 38)*
2 tablespoons ground Sichuan
  peppercorns
2 star anise
4 cm (1½ inch) piece ginger,
  thickly sliced
½ cup (125 ml) vegetable oil

SEASONING

4 teaspoons light soy sauce
2 tablespoons Chinkiang
  black vinegar
5 cloves garlic, minced
2 teaspoons caster (superfine) sugar

To make the chilli oil, place the chilli powder, ground Sichuan peppercorns, star anise and ginger into a heatproof bowl. Heat the vegetable oil in a small frying pan until smoking, then very carefully pour it over the spices. Leave to cool, then discard the star anise and ginger. Set aside.

Cook the noodles in a saucepan of boiling water according to the packet instructions, then drain and immerse in iced water to chill. Drain again, then add the sesame oil and stir through the noodles to prevent them from sticking together.

To make the seasoning, combine the light soy sauce, Chinkiang vinegar, garlic and sugar in a large bowl and whisk to dissolve the sugar. Add the chilli oil, then toss the noodles through the sauce to combine thoroughly.

Divide the dressed noodles between four bowls, top with the sesame seeds, cucumber and spring onion, and serve.

GOLDEN SHRIMP ROE NOODLES

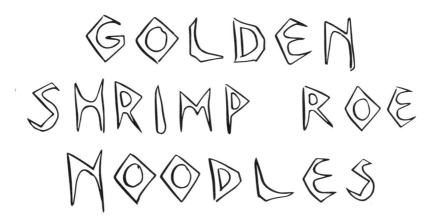

Dried shrimp roe can be found in the fridge or freezer section of your local Asian grocer. These tiny orange specks pack an absolute wallop of punchy umami flavour, so much so that this dish requires little else. The oyster sauce and lard simply help to coat the noodles and distribute the flavour.

SERVES 4

400 g (14 oz) fresh thin egg noodles
2 tablespoons lard
  (see Notes on page 28)
1 tablespoon oyster sauce
2 tablespoons dried shrimp roe

Cook the noodles in a saucepan of boiling water until al dente, 1–2 minutes.

Meanwhile, warm the lard in a small frying pan and combine with the oyster sauce.

Drain the noodles into a large mixing bowl and pour the lard mixture over the top. Mix thoroughly, adding more oyster sauce if required.

Divide the noodles between four bowls, sprinkle the shrimp roe over the top and serve.

Wonton Noodle Soup

ON MY LAST VISIT TO HONG KONG, I CHANCED UPON A NOODLE SHOP THAT STILL MADE THEIR NOODLES USING THE TRADITIONAL METHOD, WHERE THE CHEF BOUNCES ON A THICK BAMBOO POLE TO WORK THE DUCK-EGG-ENRICHED DOUGH TO ITS OPTIMAL CONSISTENCY. THIS LABORIOUS PROCESS RESULTS IN THE MOST PERFECT, SPRINGY, TOOTHSOME NOODLES. TRADITIONALLY, THESE NOODLES ARE SERVED WITH PORK AND PRAWN WONTONS IN A DELICIOUS AND FLAVOURFUL BROTH, THE BEST WAY TO APPRECIATE THEIR SIMPLE PERFECTION.

WHILST TRADITIONALLY MADE EGG NOODLES AREN'T AS READILY AVAILABLE AS I'D LIKE, THE JOY OF A COMFORTING BOWL OF WONTON NOODLE SOUP IS STILL VERY MUCH WITHIN REACH. IF YOU'RE NOT MAKING YOUR OWN STOCK, BUY A GOOD-QUALITY ONE, AND LOOK FOR FRESH EGG NOODLES IN THE FRIDGE SECTION OF YOUR LOCAL ASIAN GROCER.

WHEN I MAKE WONTONS, I USUALLY TRY TO MAKE ENOUGH TO FREEZE SOME FOR LATER, READY TO PULL OUT AND HEAT UP ON A WHIM. PRETTY CLOUDS OF WONTONS FLOATING IN A FRAGRANT BROTH WITH A TANGLE OF PERFECTLY AL DENTE EGG NOODLES, ALL OF WHICH CAN BE EASILY KNOCKED TOGETHER IN LESS THAN 15 MINUTES? YES, PLEASE!

— EGG NOODLES —

SERVES 4

8 cups (2 litres) stock (see page 51),
    or use a good-quality
    store-bought stock
Salt, to taste
300 g (10½ oz) fresh egg noodles
24 wontons (see pages 57, 58)
½ bunch bok choy, halved lengthways
    and blanched
2 teaspoons sesame oil
½ teaspoon ground white pepper
4 spring onions (scallions) or
    garlic chives, sliced

Bring the stock to the boil in a large saucepan or stockpot and season with salt. Add the noodles and wontons and boil until the wontons float to the top and the noodles are al dente. Drain the wontons and noodles and divide them evenly between four bowls, reserving the hot stock.

Divide the blanched bok choy and hot stock between the bowls and top with sesame oil, white pepper, and the spring onions or garlic chives. Serve immediately.

Chongqing Hot and Sour Noodles

Also known as *'suan la fen'* (酸辣粉), this Sichuan street food dish of bouncy potato noodles in a sour and numbing broth is flavourful, textural, bright, fresh and packed full of toppings. All you need are some basic Chinese pantry ingredients to build this bowl of seriously good times.

SERVES 4

200 g (7 oz) dried sweet potato or mung bean (cellophane) noodles *(see Note)*, soaked in cold water for 1 hour to soften and then drained
2 tablespoons vegetable oil
4 cloves garlic, minced
1 teaspoon ground Sichuan peppercorns
1 teaspoon five spice powder
¼ cup (60 ml) chilli oil (see page 94), or use Lao Gan Ma chilli oil)
¼ cup (60 ml) light soy sauce
⅓ cup (80 ml) Chinkiang black vinegar
2 cups (500 ml) hot stock (see page 51), or use a good-quality store-bought stock
4 spring onions (scallions), sliced
⅓ cup (50 g) *ya cai* (see Notes on page 38)
2 tablespoons roasted peanuts
1 tablespoon sesame seeds
Handful of coriander (cilantro) sprigs, finely chopped

Cook the softened noodles in a saucepan of boiling water until tender, 8–10 minutes. They will still be chewy, but should be fully translucent when cooked. Drain and rinse with warm water, drain again and set aside.

Heat the vegetable oil in a small frying pan over medium heat. Add the garlic and stir-fry until fragrant. Add the ground Sichuan peppercorns, five spice powder, chilli oil and light soy sauce and stir. Remove from the heat and add the Chinkiang vinegar.

Divide this sauce between four bowls. Divide the noodles between the bowls and top each with a ladle of hot stock, and some spring onion, *ya cai*, peanuts, sesame seeds and coriander. Serve immediately.

NOTE
You can find dried sweet potato or mung bean (cellophane) noodles in the Asian aisle of well-stocked supermarkets or at most Asian grocers.

'ANTS CLIMBING A TREE' NOODLES

This is one of my favourite Sichuan dishes. It's a very charming example of a dish named after the story behind it, the tale of an impoverished heroine who cooked a meal for her sick mother-in-law, only to be asked why there were ants all over it (the 'ants' being the minced pork stuck to the noodle threads). Call it what you will, there's no denying these noodles are incredibly tasty.

SERVES 4

2 tablespoons vegetable oil
200 g (7 oz) pork mince
   (ground pork)
2 tablespoons *doubanjiang*
   (see Note)
4 cloves garlic, minced
4 cm (1½ inch) piece ginger, minced
4 spring onions (scallions), sliced,
   green and white parts separated
3 cups (750 ml) stock (see page 51),
   or use a good-quality
   store-bought stock
350 g (12 oz) mung bean (cellophane)
   noodles *(see Note on page 46)*,
   soaked in cold water for 1 hour to
   soften and then drained
2 teaspoons caster (superfine) sugar
2 tablespoons light soy sauce

Heat 1 tablespoon oil in a wok or frying pan over medium heat and fry the pork mince until golden. Push the pork to the side of the pan and add the remaining oil, *doubanjiang*, garlic, ginger and sliced white spring onion and stir-fry until aromatic. Toss the pork through this sauce, then pour the stock over and bring to the boil.

Add the softened mung bean noodles, sugar and light soy sauce and stir to combine, 2–3 minutes. Transfer to a plate, sprinkle with green spring onion and serve immediately.

NOTE
Doubanjiang, a spicy fermented bean sauce, can be found in the Asian aisle of well-stocked supermarkets, or at most Asian grocers.

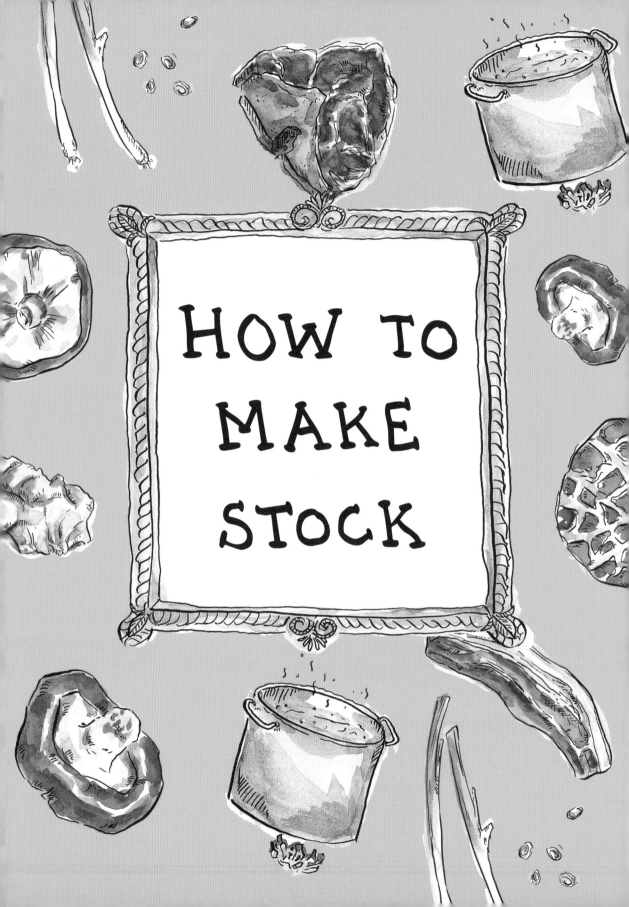

HOW TO MAKE STOCK

CHINESE EVERYDAY STOCK

This is the basic stock used in Chinese cooking, referred to simply as 'stock' throughout this book. It functions as the soup for noodle dishes when seasoned, a sauce for stir-fries when thickened, and as a cooking liquid for congee. A teaspoon here and there is also used to enrich dipping sauces. Most versions of Chinese stock include pork bones but, for simplicity's sake, I've omitted them here and given pork stock its own separate recipe.

MAKES 4 CUPS (1 LITRE)

500 g (1 lb 2 oz) chicken wings
   or carcasses
4 cm (1½ inch) piece ginger,
   skin on, sliced
2 spring onions (scallions), halved

Place the chicken in a large saucepan or stockpot and cover with 12 cups (3 litres) water. Slowly bring to the boil, then reduce the heat to low and simmer for 20 minutes. Skim any scum or impurities from the surface and add the ginger and spring onion. Partially cover the pan and simmer for 2 hours, skimming occasionally. Allow to cool, then strain the stock, discarding the solids.

Chill the stock overnight and remove the layer of fat that forms on the surface. You can keep this fat to cook with later. The stock will keep in the fridge for 5 days, or for up to 3 months in the freezer.

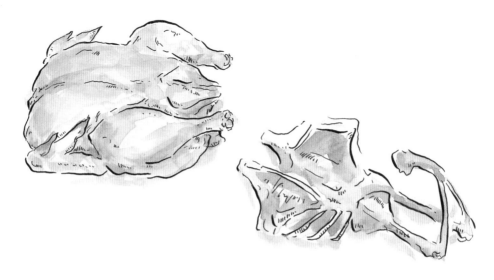

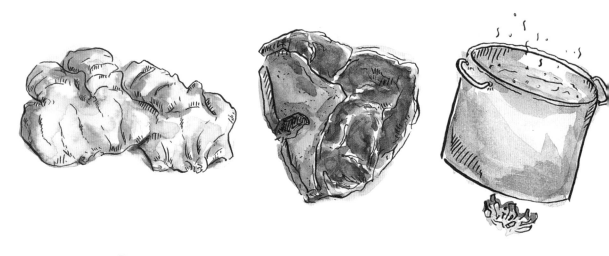

PORK STOCK

A BOWL OF SOUP IS A PERMANENT FIXTURE ON THE CHINESE
DINNER TABLE — A PRODUCT OF FRUGALITY, BUT ALSO A WAY TO
ENSURE THAT ALL THE NUTRIENTS FROM EACH INGREDIENT ARE
CONSUMED. PORK BONES ARE PARTICULARLY FLAVOURFUL AND
ARE OFTEN MORE AFFORDABLE THAN CHICKEN BONES, MAKING
THEM A RICH YET ECONOMICAL OPTION FOR SOUPS AND STEWS.
THIS STOCK CAN ALSO BE USED TO ENHANCE DISHES. FOR A CLEAR
STOCK WITH A CLEAN FLAVOUR, IT IS IMPORTANT TO BLANCH THE
BONES BEFOREHAND TO REMOVE ANY IMPURITIES. THE BLANCHING
PROCESS IS INTEGRAL TO STOCK-MAKING WHEN USING BONES FROM
LARGE ANIMALS.

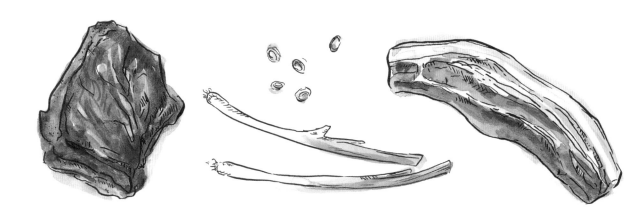

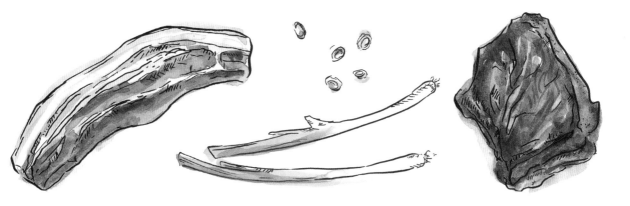

MAKES 4 CUPS (1 LITRE)

2 kg (4 lb 8 oz) pork neck bones
500 g (1 lb 2 oz) pork spareribs
5 cm (2 inch) piece ginger,
    skin on, sliced
2 spring onions (scallions), halved
200 ml (7 fl oz) Shaoxing wine

Place the pork bones and spareribs into a large saucepan or stockpot and pour in enough water to cover. Bring to the boil over high heat and blanch for 8–10 minutes. Discard the blanching water and rinse the bones thoroughly with fresh water. Clean the saucepan to remove any scum, then return the rinsed bones to the saucepan. Cover with fresh water and repeat the blanching and rinsing process.

Once you have blanched the bones a second time, fill the cleaned saucepan with 12 cups (3 litres) cold water, along with the blanched bones, ginger, spring onions and Shaoxing wine. Bring to the boil over high heat. Skim any impurities that appear on the surface during the first 10–15 minutes, then reduce the heat to low and simmer for 4–5 hours, skimming occasionally.

Allow the stock to cool, then strain, discarding the solids. Chill overnight and remove the layer of fat that forms on the surface. You can keep this fat to cook with later. The stock will keep in the fridge for 5 days, or for up to 3 months in the freezer.

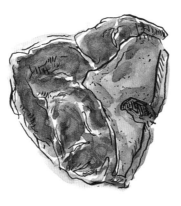

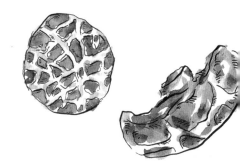

vegetarian stock

This recipe is for a flavourful stock that will need to be seasoned further if you wish to serve it as a soup. Don't be tempted to add soy sauce, because the flavour from the shiitake mushrooms and the umami from the kombu are beautiful and need only some gentle enhancement with salt. I repeat: no soy! Start this stock the night before.

MAKES 4 CUPS (1 LITRE)

50 g (1¾ oz) dried shiitake
    mushrooms
8 cups (2 litres) water
2 large pieces dried kombu, or
    70 g (2½ oz) kombu extract
5 cm (2 inch) piece ginger,
    skin on, sliced
2½ teaspoons salt

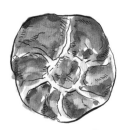

Soak the shiitake mushrooms overnight in enough cold water to cover, ensuring you weigh them down with something, such as a small bowl. If you're in a rush, just soak them in warm water for 20–30 minutes or until they're nice and soft. Reserve both the shiitake-infused water and the shiitake mushrooms.

If using whole kombu pieces, soak them overnight in a large saucepan or stockpot with 4 cups (1 litre) cold water. The next day, place the saucepan with the kombu and water on the stove, add another 4 cups (1 litre) water and slowly bring to the boil. Just before it starts to boil, remove the kombu and add the shiitake mushrooms and shiitake-infused water. Add the ginger and reduce the heat to low. Simmer for 2–3 hours, until the broth has reduced by half. Season with the salt, then strain the stock, discarding the solids. Allow to cool.

If using kombu extract, place the water, kombu extract, shiitake mushrooms and shiitake-infused water in a large saucepan or stockpot and bring to the boil. Add the ginger and reduce the heat to low. Simmer for 2–3 hours, until the broth has reduced by half. Season with the salt, then strain the stock, discarding the solids. Allow to cool.

The stock will keep in the fridge for 5 days, or for up to 3 months in the freezer.

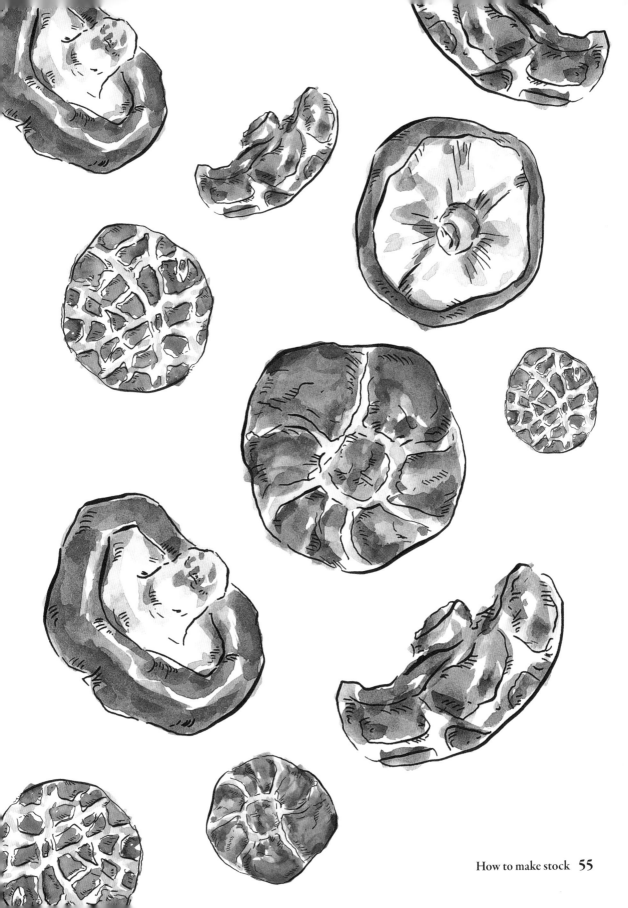

HOW TO MAKE WONTONS

A WONTON IS A DUMPLING, BUT NOT ALL DUMPLINGS ARE WONTONS. THEY ARE NOT INTERCHANGEABLE, AND WONTONS HAVE SPECIFIC FORMS, FOLDS, FILLINGS AND SERVING STYLES. TO CONFUSE THE TWO WOULD BE UNWISE. SERVE YOUR WONTONS HOWEVER YOU LIKE, OR IN ONE OF THE THREE WAYS SUGGESTED ON PAGE 60.

VEGETARIAN WONTONS

Shiitake mushrooms, black fungus and fried tofu puffs provide a delightfully textural stand-in for the classic pork and prawn wonton filling over the page. Wonton wrappers come in white and yellow varieties and some are vegan. It is unwise to substitute wonton wrappers with normal dumpling or gyoza wrappers, which are too thick.

MAKES 40

40 wonton wrappers

FILLING
100 g (3½ oz) fresh shiitake mushrooms, finely chopped
100 g (3½ oz) dried black fungus (wood-ear mushrooms), soaked in hot water until soft and then finely chopped
4 x 5 cm (2 inch) pieces fried tofu puffs *(see Notes)*, finely chopped
5 garlic chives, finely chopped
3 cm (1¼ inch) piece ginger, finely chopped
½ teaspoon cornflour (cornstarch)
1 teaspoon sesame oil
½ tablespoon light soy sauce
½ tablespoon salt
¼ teaspoon ground white pepper

Mix all of the filling ingredients together in a large bowl until well combined, then leave to rest in the fridge for 30 minutes.

Place 1 teaspoon of filling in the centre of a wonton wrapper. Using your fingertip, moisten the edges with a little water, fold the wrapper over to enclose the filling and pinch to seal. Repeat with the remaining filling and wrappers.

Bring a large saucepan of water to the boil and add the wontons in batches of 10. Return to the boil. Once the wontons float to the surface, continue to cook them for a further 3 minutes, then use a slotted spoon to transfer them to a serving bowl.

NOTES
Fried tofu puffs can be found in the fridge and freezer sections of most Asian grocers. Wontons can be made in batches ahead of time and frozen for up to a month.

PORK AND PRAWN WONTONS

When I think of wontons, I think fondly of this classic pork and prawn filling.
Bouncy, savoury and super tasty, sometimes you just don't mess with perfection.

MAKES 40

40 wonton wrappers

FILLING
200 g (7 oz) pork mince
  (ground pork)
70 g (2½ oz) raw prawns (shrimp),
  peeled, deveined and
  finely chopped
1 egg
2 spring onions (scallions),
  finely chopped
1 teaspoon finely chopped ginger
1 teaspoon sesame oil
2 teaspoons light soy sauce
2 teaspoons salt
¼ teaspoon ground white pepper

Mix all of the filling ingredients together in a large bowl until
well combined, then leave to rest in the fridge for 30 minutes.

Place 1 teaspoon of filling in the centre of a wonton wrapper.
Using your fingertip, moisten the edges with a little water, fold
the wrapper over to enclose the filling and pinch to seal. Repeat
with the remaining filling and wrappers.

Bring a large saucepan of water to the boil and add the wontons
in batches of 10. Return to the boil. Once the wontons float to the
surface, continue to cook them for a further 3 minutes, then use
a slotted spoon to transfer them to a serving bowl.

NOTE
Wontons can be made in batches ahead of time and frozen for up
to a month.

TRIANGULAR INGOT

RUFFLED PURSE

RECTANGULAR INGOT

POUCH

WONTONS, THREE WAYS

ENVELOPE

EACH SERVES 1–2

IN BROTH

2 cups (500 ml) hot stock
   (see page 51)
1 teaspoon salt
¼ teaspoon ground white pepper
1 tablespoon chopped spring
   onion (scallion)
8–12 hot boiled wontons
   (see pages 57, 58)
Blanched leafy green vegetables,
   to serve

Season the stock with the salt
and white pepper. Add the spring
onion, hot boiled wontons and
blanched leafy green vegetables
and serve.

IN SICHUAN RED OIL DRESSING

2 tablespoons chilli oil
   (see page 94, or use Lao
   Gan Ma chilli oil)
1 teaspoon light soy sauce
1 tablespoon Chinkiang
   black vinegar
1 tablespoon sesame oil
1 teaspoon finely chopped garlic
1 teaspoon finely chopped ginger
8–12 hot boiled wontons
   (see pages 57, 58)
Toasted sesame seeds and sliced
   spring onion (scallion), to serve

Mix the chilli oil, light soy sauce,
Chinkiang vinegar, sesame oil,
garlic and ginger together to
combine. Pour the dressing over
the hot boiled wontons, garnish
with sesame seeds and sliced
spring onion and serve.

DEEP-FRIED

Vegetable oil, for deep-frying
8–12 uncooked wontons
   (see pages 57, 58)
Store-bought sweet and sour
   sauce, to serve

Heat the vegetable oil to 180°C
(350°F) using a food thermometer
to check the temperature, and
deep-fry the wontons in batches
for 2–3 minutes, until crisp and
golden. Serve with sweet and
sour sauce.

FISH-SHAPED

NURSE CAP

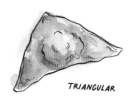

TRIANGULAR

HOW TO MAKE DUMPLINGS

JO'S MUM'S DUMPLINGS
(DUMPLINGS BY XIAOLING)

JO: This endeavour started with the best of intentions. I have often proclaimed that when it comes to dumplings, I have never tried a restaurant version that beat my mum's homemade ones, so we thought this would be a fitting inclusion in this chapter. Sounds great, I thought – I'll just go home and ask her for her recipe. Easier said than done.

I can't be alone in the discovery that trying to write down a family recipe in quantifiable terms is, in fact, a momentous feat. There are, apparently, no such things as measurements.

'Well, *how much* oyster sauce?'

'I don't know, I just do *this*.' Mum makes a sauce-pouring gesture with her hand.

And the whole process seems to be peppered with unjustifiable steps steeped purely in superstition. According to my mum, the dumpling filling should always be stirred anticlockwise only.

'*Why?*'

'Because Chinese people do everything anticlockwise.'

One stressful afternoon of gathering ingredients and attempting to weigh and record them all later, I finally managed to transcribe the following recipe.

DUMPLING FILLING

JO : Dumpling fillings come down to personal preference, and I believe there are no wrong combinations. This is simply the way I remember making them with my family for special occasions such as Chinese New Year, which grants them a special place in my heart. The generosity with which prawns (shrimp) and ginger are added sets these apart from any dumplings you could buy at a shop.

**MAKES ENOUGH FOR
50–60 DUMPLINGS**

1 tablespoon Sichuan peppercorns
½ cup (125 ml) hot water
300 g (10½ oz) pork mince
　(ground pork)
150 g (5½ oz) chicken mince
　(ground chicken)
1 tablespoon finely chopped ginger
Pinch of salt
1 teaspoon ground white pepper
1½ tablespoons light soy sauce
3 teaspoons oyster sauce
200 g (7 oz) raw prawns (shrimp),
　peeled, deveined and
　coarsely chopped
200 g (7 oz) garlic chives,
　finely chopped
2 teaspoons vegetable oil
1 egg, lightly beaten
2 teaspoons sesame oil

Soak the Sichuan peppercorns in the hot water to infuse the water with flavour. Wait until the water is almost cold before starting the dumpling filling. Strain out the peppercorns to use at another time, and reserve the infused water.

To make the dumpling filling, mix the pork and chicken mince together in a large bowl to combine. Add the ginger and mix through, then slowly add the infused water little by little, mixing well after each addition. The mixture should start to resemble a paste. Season the dumpling filling according to your own taste. We suggest starting with a generous pinch of salt, ½ teaspoon white pepper, 1 tablespoon soy sauce and 2 teaspoons oyster sauce, and mixing thoroughly. If in doubt, place a small amount on a plate and microwave for 10–15 seconds to cook the mince, then taste.

Combine the prawns with the remaining ½ tablespoon soy sauce, ½ teaspoon white pepper and 1 teaspoon oyster sauce, then incorporate them into the meat mixture. You can repeat the process of microwaving and tasting a small amount if you're uncertain about the seasoning. The dumpling filling should be adequately salty because once wrapped and cooked, it will taste less salty.

Add the garlic chives and vegetable oil. Let the oil roughly coat the garlic chives before fully incorporating them into the filling. Add the egg and sesame oil and mix to combine, then assemble your dumplings (see over the page).

DUMPLING WRAPPERS

JO : There is absolutely no shame in purchasing ready-made dumpling wrappers –
they're a great time-saver in the already time-consuming process of making
dumplings from scratch. However, making your own wrappers isn't too difficult
once you master rolling out the dough.

MAKES 60

2⅔ cups (400 g) plain
   (all-purpose) flour
1 teaspoon salt

Place all of the ingredients in a bowl with 1 cup (250 ml) water
and mix together by hand or with a stand mixer until an elastic
dough forms. Leave to rest for 15–20 minutes.

Roll the dough out into a log, roughly 3–4 cm (1¼–1½ inches)
in diameter. Cut into 1–2 cm (½–¾ inch) pieces, ready to roll into
individual dumpling wrappers. The technique used here is to spin
the dough with one hand while working the rolling pin with the
other on a lightly-floured benchtop, rolling outwards from the
centre to flatten the dough and not stretch it. You're aiming for a
circular shape of a few millimetres thickness, but a more rectangular
shape is also fine.

HOW TO ASSEMBLE YOUR DUMPLINGS
Spoon some of the dumpling filling onto a wrapper – the
amount will vary depending on the size of the wrapper. Ideally,
you want about 1.5 cm (⅝ inch) between the filling and the
wrapper edge. If in doubt, start small and work your way up.
Fold the wrapper over the filling. If using store-bought
wrappers, you will need a bowl of water on the side to dip your
finger in to seal the edges. If using fresh wrappers, this won't be
necessary as the dough will be pliable enough to seal simply by
pinching it closed. You want to make sure the whole edge is
sealed well to avoid the dumplings breaking apart in the water.
Repeat with the remaining filling and wrappers.

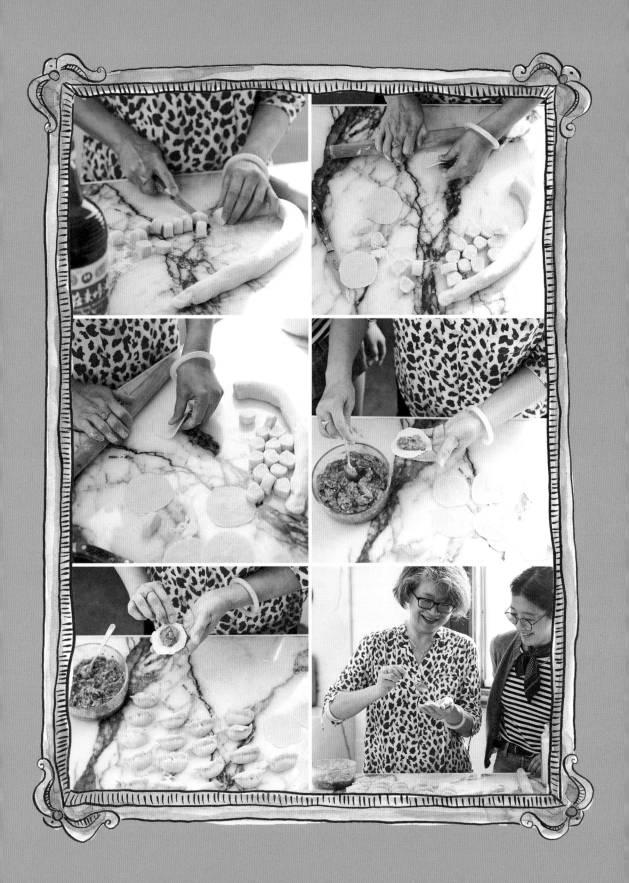

HOW TO COOK YOUR DUMPLINGS

JO: BRING A LARGE SAUCEPAN OF WATER UP TO A GENTLE BOIL AND CAREFULLY LOWER A BATCH OF DUMPLINGS INTO THE SAUCEPAN. HAVE A STRAINER OR SIEVE ON HAND TO GIVE THE DUMPLINGS A GENTLE STIR IMMEDIATELY AFTER THEY'RE SUBMERGED TO ENSURE THEY DON'T STICK TO EACH OTHER OR THE BOTTOM OF THE PAN. TRY NOT TO OVERLOAD THE PAN – MOST HOMES ONLY HAVE SAUCEPANS BIG ENOUGH TO REQUIRE MULTIPLE BATCHES OF DUMPLING COOKING. WHEN THE WATER RETURNS TO THE BOIL, ADD A CUP OF COLD WATER. ONCE THE WATER IS BOILING AGAIN, ADD ONE MORE CUP OF COLD WATER. WHEN IT RETURNS TO THE BOIL, YOUR DUMPLINGS WILL BE READY TO BE FISHED OUT WITH A SIEVE AND EATEN.

YOU CAN EAT THE DUMPLINGS WITH ANY CONDIMENTS YOU LIKE. MY FAMILY ENJOYS A DIPPING SAUCE OF CHINKIANG BLACK VINEGAR AND SLICED FRESH CHILLI. AFTER EVERYONE HAS FINISHED EATING THE DUMPLINGS, THERE IS A CUSTOM OF POURING SOME OF THE DUMPLING-COOKING WATER INTO YOUR BOWL TO COMBINE WITH ANY LEFT-OVER VINEGAR AND CHILLI AND THEN DRINKING THIS AS A BROTH. IT'S ALSO KNOWN AS 'SOUP TO DIGEST THE STARCH' (原汤化原食). THIS IS TOTALLY OPTIONAL, OF COURSE: I'VE ALWAYS DECLINED THIS PART OF THE MEAL, BUT I'M ALSO SOMEONE WHO DISLIKES CEREAL MILK, SO MAYBE I'M THE ANOMALY HERE.

HERE ARE A COUPLE MORE SUGGESTIONS FOR DUMPLING FILLINGS, INCLUDING ONE INSPIRED BY A VERY FAMOUS RESTAURANT IN MELBOURNE, KNOWN FOR THEIR VERY MELBOURNE-FLAVOURED DUMPLINGS. SIMPLY COMBINE ALL THE FILLING INGREDIENTS WELL, THEN FOLLOW THE SAME ASSEMBLY STEPS AS THE PREVIOUS RECIPE (PAGE 66).

PORK AND CHIVE
MAKES 50–60

500 g (1 lb 2 oz) pork mince (ground pork)
400 g (14 oz) garlic chives, finely chopped
1 egg, lightly beaten
⅓ cup (80 ml) light soy sauce
¼ cup (60 ml) sesame oil
½ teaspoon ground white pepper

EGG AND BLACK FUNGUS
MAKES 50–60

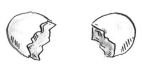

300 g (10½ oz) cooked scrambled eggs
200 g (7 oz) dried black fungus (wood-ear mushrooms), soaked in hot water until soft and then finely chopped
200 g (7 oz) garlic chives, finely chopped
⅓ cup (80 ml) light soy sauce
1 teaspoon five spice powder
½ teaspoon ground white pepper

SHANDONG MAMA-INSPIRED
FISH AND DILL
MAKES 50–60

500 g (1 lb 2 oz) Spanish mackerel meat, bones and skin removed
100 g (3½ oz) pork mince (ground pork)
50 g (1¾ oz) garlic chives, finely chopped
50 g (1¾ oz) dill sprigs, finely chopped
100 ml (3½ fl oz) Shaoxing wine
⅓ cup (80 ml) light soy sauce
1 tablespoon fish sauce
4 cm (1½ inch) piece ginger, finely chopped
½ teaspoon ground white pepper

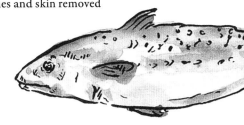

HOW TO MAKE FRIED RICE

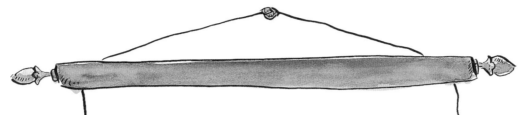

THERE ARE SOME KEY POINTS TO TAKE NOTE
OF HERE, BEARING IN MIND THAT I AM
REFERRING SPECIFICALLY TO CHINESE-STYLE
FRIED RICE. THIS IS SOMETHING I FEEL QUITE
STRONGLY ABOUT, SO FORGIVE THE RANT.

1 **ALWAYS** use left-over rice that has had time to dry out in the fridge or freezer (ensuring you cool and store cooked rice properly to avoid contamination). This way, the grains will be nice and dry and will fluff up again with the heat of the wok. It's called stir-*frying,* not stir-*steaming.* Break up any lumps of rice with a spatula or your fingers before cooking.

2 **BE GENTLE.** The next time you eat at a Chinese restaurant, take a close look at your fried rice. Are the grains intact or smashed up? Are they individually fluffed and separated? If so, that's the sign of an excellent wok chef. If not, and your fried rice is smashed into oblivion, you're looking at the work of an amateur.

3 **DON'T OVERCROWD YOUR WOK OR PAN.** My snarky comment about frying versus steaming applies here, too. You need sufficient space to move the rice and ingredients around, keeping the temperature high enough that the ingredients fry (not stew) and then steam in the hot pan.

4 **CUT YOUR INGREDIENTS INTO SMALL PIECES AND PRE-COOK PROTEINS.** You want the whole dish to be ready in less than 5 minutes. As a general rule of thumb, proteins should always be pre-cooked. Choose vegetables that will cook quickly in the pan – the less moisture you add to your fried rice, the tastier it will be.

How to make fried rice **71**

EGG FRIED RICE

Needing no introduction, egg fried rice (炒饭) is the most basic fried rice in the Chinese repertoire. Consider it a jumping-off point for other variations and a base for adding any other ingredients you wish. Once you can successfully cook egg fried rice, you'll be able to nail every other version, too.

SERVES 4

2⅔ cups (500 g) day-old cooked rice
¼ cup (60 ml) vegetable oil
2 eggs
¼ teaspoon ground white pepper
2 teaspoons salt
1 teaspoon caster (superfine) sugar
1 teaspoon MSG (optional, *see Note*)
2 spring onions (scallions),
    sliced into rounds

Very gently break up any lumps of rice with a spatula or your fingers, taking care to keep the individual grains intact. Allow the rice to come to room temperature.

Heat the vegetable oil in a wok or frying pan over medium heat. When the oil is hot, add the eggs and stir quickly. Make a well in the centre of the partially-cooked eggs and add the rice. Stir the rice through the eggs, continuing to break up any lumps you find. You want to distribute the egg through the rice as evenly as possible.

Continue to cook the rice over medium–high heat until the grains fluff up again from the steam. The key is to control the heat – don't let the grains burn or colour in any way. Be patient.

When the rice is ready and starting to sizzle, add the white pepper, salt, sugar and MSG (if using) and stir through. Add the spring onion and cook for 1 minute or so before serving.

NOTE
MSG is a flavour enhancer used in East Asian cooking to intensify savouriness, and provide body and balance to some dishes. It is naturally occurring in some cheeses, seaweed and tomatoes. You can find it at most Asian grocers.

VEGETABLE FRIED RICE

This is a delicious way to use up any sad-looking green vegetables in your fridge. Once you've mastered the technique for preparing this fried rice, you can add anything and everything you like. I maintain that the stems are the tastiest parts of leafy green vegetables. Make this and you'll probably agree.

SERVES 4

2⅔ cups (500 g) day-old cooked rice
2 tablespoons vegetable oil
4 gai lan (Chinese broccoli) or broccolini (sprouting broccoli) stems, sliced into rounds
¼ teaspoon ground white pepper
2 teaspoons salt
1 teaspoon caster (superfine) sugar
1 teaspoon MSG (optional) (*see Note on page 72*)
3 spring onions (scallions), sliced into rounds

Very gently break up any lumps of rice with a spatula or your fingers, taking care to keep the individual grains intact. Allow the rice to come to room temperature.

Heat the vegetable oil in a wok or frying pan over medium heat. When the oil is hot, add the rice and stir, breaking up any lumps as you fry. Continue to cook the rice over medium–high heat until the grains fluff up again from the steam. The key is to control the heat – don't let the grains burn or colour in any way. Be patient.

When the rice is ready and starting to sizzle, add the gai lan or broccolini stems and fry until bright jade-green. Stir to distribute the greens through the rice, then add the white pepper, salt, sugar and MSG (if using). Add the spring onion and cook for 1 minute or so before serving.

billionaire fried rice

Billionaire fried rice (瑶柱旦白炒饭), otherwise known as 'big shot fried rice' or 'generosity fried rice', is a fixture at high-end Chinese banquets. It's named after the mysterious Hong Kong billionaire who is credited with its creation, and its name befits its prestige (in case anyone missed the 'billionaire' reference). This is a fried rice like no other, with golden shreds of scallop peeking through glossy rice grains, surrounded by soft clouds of egg white, and topped with little orange bursts of roe. This is the Rolls-Royce of fried rice dishes, yet it only uses a handful of ingredients.

The star of this dish is *conpoy*, or dried scallop, a luxury ingredient in Cantonese cooking that is notoriously expensive. These little nuggets pack an incredibly concentrated oceanic, umami flavour, and are a key component of XO sauce.

Luckily for us non-billionaires, *conpoy* is available in various sizes and grades and as with all dehydrated seafood, a little goes a long way. The smaller size will do just fine in this recipe – just ensure it isn't too hard and dry. A completely acceptable and more affordable version can be found in vacuum-sealed bags at most Asian grocers. The *conpoy* needs to be rehydrated overnight before use, so make sure you read this recipe from start to finish before you start cooking. You can up the ante by adding other luxe ingredients like cooked lobster, crab and fish roe, but the *conpoy* should be front and centre.

SERVES 4

1 teaspoon Shaoxing wine
5–6 *conpoy* (dried scallops)
2 tablespoons vegetable oil
3 egg whites
2⅔ cups (500 g) day-old
    cooked rice
5 gai lan (Chinese broccoli) or
    broccolini (sprouting broccoli)
    stems, sliced into rounds
60 g (2¼ oz) cooked crab meat
    (optional)
1 teaspoon salt
15 g (½ oz) flying fish roe
    (optional)

The night before, combine 2 cups (500 ml) water with the Shaoxing wine in a small bowl and submerge the dried scallops in the mixture. Cover and allow to stand overnight in the fridge to rehydrate, or on the bench if your kitchen is cool.

The next day, drain the rehydrated scallops and pat dry. Shred into small pieces and set aside.

Heat 1 tablespoon oil in a wok or frying pan over medium heat and fry the shredded scallop until golden. Remove from the pan and set aside.

Heat the remaining oil in the pan over medium–high heat, until smoking. Add the egg whites and stir quickly to scramble. Add the rice and toss to combine, distributing the egg through the rice. Continue to stir-fry the rice and egg, until the rice begins to soften.

Add the gai lan or broccolini stems and fried scallop and continue to cook over medium–high heat until the rice grains are hot and fluffy. If you're using crab meat, add it now.

Once the rice is fluffy and starting to sizzle, and the gai lan or broccolini stems are bright jade-green, add the salt and toss to combine. Transfer to a plate and top with flying fish roe, if using. Serve immediately.

NOTE
If you forget to rehydrate the dried scallops overnight, you can submerge them in the same volume of water and Shaoxing wine and nuke them in the microwave on high for 1 minute. Allow them to stand for 10–15 minutes, then drain, pat dry and shred.

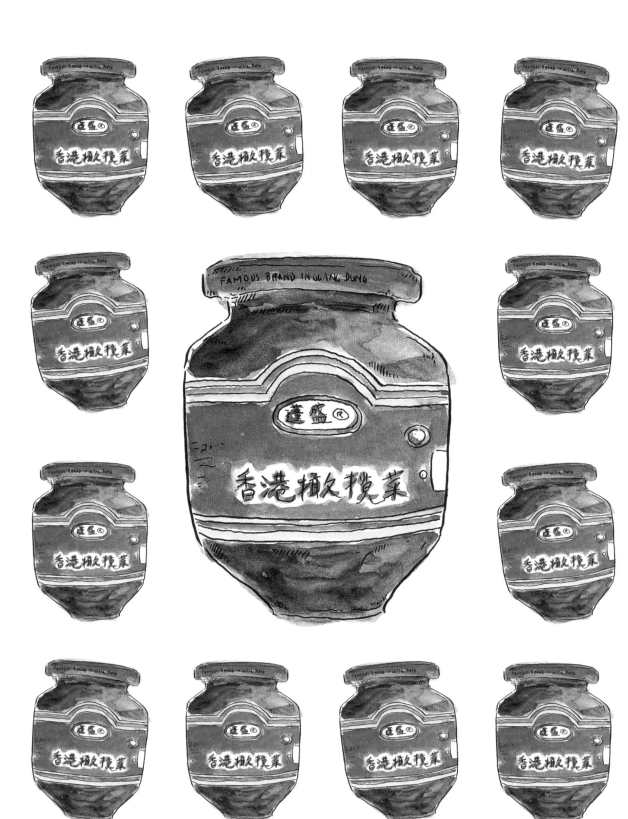

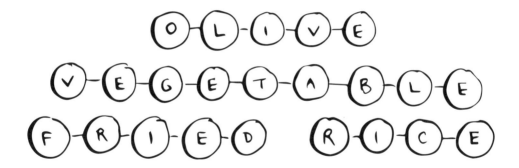

OLIVE VEGETABLE FRIED RICE

Preserved olive vegetable is my favourite condiment. It's a Teochew specialty of mustard greens and green olives preserved in soy sauce and oil – and it's incredibly savoury, lending depth of flavour to this fried rice. My family often visits a Buddhist vegetarian restaurant in Singapore where they make the most wonderful olive fried rice with jade-green broccoli stems. It's so simple and delicious! A really excellent Thai version of this fried rice also exists, using Chinese salted black olives. It's seasoned with a little fish sauce, spiked with birdseye chilli and served with shallots and coriander (cilantro). This recipe mashes all of the versions I love together and is comprehensive enough to serve as a complete meal.

SERVES 4

¼ cup (60 ml) vegetable oil
2 eggs
1 tablespoon shrimp paste
2 small French or Asian shallots, minced
3 cloves garlic, minced
100 g (3½ oz) pork or chicken mince (ground pork or chicken)
¼ cup (50 g) preserved olive vegetable
2⅔ cups (500 g) day-old cooked rice
1 teaspoon fish sauce
½ teaspoon salt
½ teaspoon caster (superfine) sugar
1 birdseye chilli, thinly sliced
Sliced coriander (cilantro) leaves, sliced French or Asian shallot and lime wedges, to serve

Heat 1 tablespoon oil in a wok or frying pan over medium heat and cook the eggs, scrambling them into fluffy clouds. Remove the scrambled eggs while still soft and set aside.

Wipe the wok clean and heat the remaining oil over medium heat. Add the shrimp paste and fry until it smells wonderfully fragrant, then add the shallots and fry for 20–30 seconds over medium–high heat. Add the garlic and fry until it begins to soften.

Add the pork or chicken mince and continue to stir-fry, keeping the pan moving as you break the mince into smaller pieces with your spatula. Fry the mince until it begins to crisp up and turn golden, 4–5 minutes.

Add the olive vegetable and rice, gently incorporating the crisped pork, shallots and garlic into the rice without breaking the grains. Fry until the rice starts to sizzle, then add the fish sauce, salt and sugar and stir-fry to combine. Taste and adjust the seasoning if necessary. Add the scrambled egg and sliced birdseye chilli and fold through.

Serve the fried rice garnished with coriander leaves, sliced shallot and lime wedges.

OLIVE
VEGETABLE
FRIED RICE
SEE PAGE 79

SPECIAL
FRIED RICE
SEE PAGE 82

SPECIAL FRIED RICE

'SPECIAL FRIED RICE' (扬州炒饭) IS THE NAME USED INTERCHANGEABLY FOR YANGZHOU OR YEUNG CHOW FRIED RICE, A PROTEIN-HEAVY DISH THAT CAN BE FOUND IN MOST OVERSEAS CANTONESE RESTAURANTS. IT USES A COLOURFUL COMBINATION OF MEAT, SEAFOOD, EGG, AND VEGETABLES THAT HAVE BEEN CUT INTO TINY PIECES, IMPARTING A WORLD OF FLAVOUR WHEN FRIED WITH RICE. I PARTICULARLY LOVE THE VERSIONS FOUND IN CANTONESE BBQ RESTAURANTS, WHERE OFFCUTS OF ROAST PORK, DUCK AND CHAR SIU (CANTONESE BARBECUED PORK) IMPART A WONDERFUL SWEETNESS TO THE SMOKY, FRAGRANT RICE. THIS DISH IS A GREAT WAY TO USE UP ANY LEFT-OVER ROAST MEATS, BUT YOU COULD ALSO USE HAM OR EVEN BACON.

THE TRADITIONAL RECIPE FROM JIANGSU, A COASTAL PROVINCE NORTH OF SHANGHAI, USES RICE COOKED IN CHICKEN STOCK, WITH THE CHICKEN PIECES FINELY DICED AND COOKED THROUGH THE DISH. I USE CHICKEN BOUILLON POWDER INSTEAD TO ENRICH THE RICE. DO YOUR BEST WITH THE KNIFE WORK AND TAKE THE TIME TO CUT EVERYTHING INTO SMALL, EVEN PIECES. YOU CAN PUT ANY MEAT OR SEAFOOD YOU WANT IN THIS RICE, REALLY. JUST MAKE SURE YOU HAVE EQUAL QUANTITIES OF EACH INGREDIENT — BALANCE IS THE KEY.

SERVES 4

⅓ cup (80 ml) vegetable oil
25 g (1 oz) *char siu* (Cantonese barbecued pork), diced
25 g (1 oz) ham, diced
25 g (1 oz) Chinese roast pork, diced
25 g (1 oz) small raw prawns (shrimp), peeled and deveined
2 teaspoons Shaoxing wine
1 egg plus 1 extra yolk, whisked together
2⅔ cups (500 g) day-old cooked rice
1 teaspoon salt
1 teaspoon caster (superfine) sugar
1 teaspoon chicken bouillon powder
3 spring onions (scallions), sliced into rounds
Chilli oil (see page 94, or use Lao Gan Ma chilli oil), to serve (optional)

Heat 2 tablespoons oil in a wok or frying pan over medium heat and add the *char siu*, ham and roast pork. Stir-fry to combine, then add the prawns and stir-fry for a further 1–2 minutes. Add the Shaoxing wine and continue to stir-fry over high heat for 30 seconds. Transfer to a plate and set aside.

Wipe the wok clean and heat the remaining oil over high heat until smoking. Pour the whisked egg in and swirl the wok around to spread out the egg into a thin layer. Once the egg is partially cooked and starting to fluff up, add the rice and stir-fry, breaking up any lumps with your spatula. Fry over high heat, fluffing the rice as you go until it is sizzling.

Return the cooked meats and prawns to the wok, mixing well and continuing to fry for 1–2 minutes. Season with salt, sugar and chicken bouillon powder. Taste and adjust the seasoning if necessary. Add the sliced spring onion, stir, and serve with a big drizzle of chilli oil, if you like.

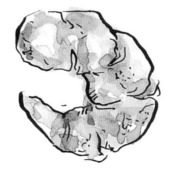

HOW TO MAKE CONGEE

PLAIN CONGEE

I had never heard the term 'congee' until we moved to Australia.
In Singapore, we called it 'porridge' and ate it for breakfast, lunch, dinner or as a snack.
Every family has their own version of this two-ingredient dish. Some like it soft and
silky, others prefer it more like a wet rice. Some eat it plain, others pile it high with
toppings. This is one of those lovely dishes where you can do no wrong.

SERVES 4

250 g (9 oz) white short-grain
    or medium-grain rice
Sprinkle each of salt, ground white
    pepper and julienned ginger,
    to serve (optional)

Wash the rice vigorously and rinse it until the water runs clear.

Bring 8 cups (2 litres) water to the boil in a large saucepan, then add
the rice. Stir and reduce the heat to a simmer. Continue cooking for
45 minutes, until the rice grains burst open and melt into the water.
Stir the congee during the last few minutes of cooking to further
break up the grains. Allow to stand for 10 minutes.

Enjoy congee hot – either just as it is – or with a sprinkle of salt,
white pepper and julienned ginger. Congee can also be served as
an accompaniment to any other dishes, or with toppings of
your choice – you are limited only by your imagination.

MUM'S CHICKEN CONGEE

Congee, or 'porridge' (see previous page), is a bowl of rice with healing powers.
My mum always made this as a remedy for coughs, colds or an upset stomach. She
strongly believes in the healing powers of ginger, and while I seriously disliked ginger
when I was younger, I now find this dish seriously delicious when sprinkled generously
with soy sauce, ginger and fragrant sesame oil. Don't forget the white pepper, either.

SERVES 4

3 chicken thigh fillets, cut into
    small pieces
2 tablespoons ginger juice *(see Note)*
¼ cup (60 ml) light soy sauce
500 g (1 lb 2 oz) plain congee
    (see page 85)

TO SERVE
1 teaspoon sesame oil
¼ teaspoon ground white pepper
1 teaspoon julienned ginger

Combine the chicken, ginger juice and soy sauce together in
a bowl and allow to stand for 15 minutes to marinate.

Place the congee in a large saucepan and bring to the boil. Add the
marinated chicken and simmer for 8 minutes, then cover and turn
the heat off. Allow to stand for 10 minutes.

Stir the congee, then divide it
between four bowls. Drizzle
with sesame oil, sprinkle with
white pepper and scatter with
julienned ginger.

NOTE
You can find ginger juice at
specialty grocers, health food
stores and most Asian grocers.

FISH CONGEE

Source the freshest fish you can find for this dish. With a recipe as simple as this one, the quality of your fish will be glaringly obvious. I also recommend avoiding freshwater fish, as the sometimes-muddy flavour can often be detected. Ling, cod or grouper, with their clean oceanic flavour, make lovely choices. My sister used to order this dish from a Cantonese restaurant we would visit in Glen Waverley in Melbourne after Saturday-morning Chinese school. I'd watch her stir in big helpings of chilli oil and soy sauce, transforming the milky-white surface into a very appetising golden-brown, dotted with pools of chilli oil. Her congee ended up being the most perfect combination of silky rice, perfectly cooked white fish, zingy fresh ginger and chilli oil.
Not one for the purists maybe, but definitely very delicious.

SERVES 4

500 g (1 lb 2 oz) plain congee
  (see page 85)
500 g (1 lb 2 oz) white fish fillets
  such as ling, cod or grouper,
  thinly sliced
1 teaspoon salt
1 spring onion (scallion), sliced
1 teaspoon julienned ginger
Soy sauce and chilli oil (see page 94,
  or use Lao Gan Ma chilli oil),
  to serve

Place the congee in a large saucepan and bring to the boil. Add the sliced fish, cover and turn off the heat. Allow to stand for 10 minutes.

Turn the heat back on to medium–low, add the salt and simmer for 3–4 minutes. The fish should be perfectly cooked. Divide the congee between four bowls and garnish with spring onion and ginger. Serve with soy sauce and chilli oil.

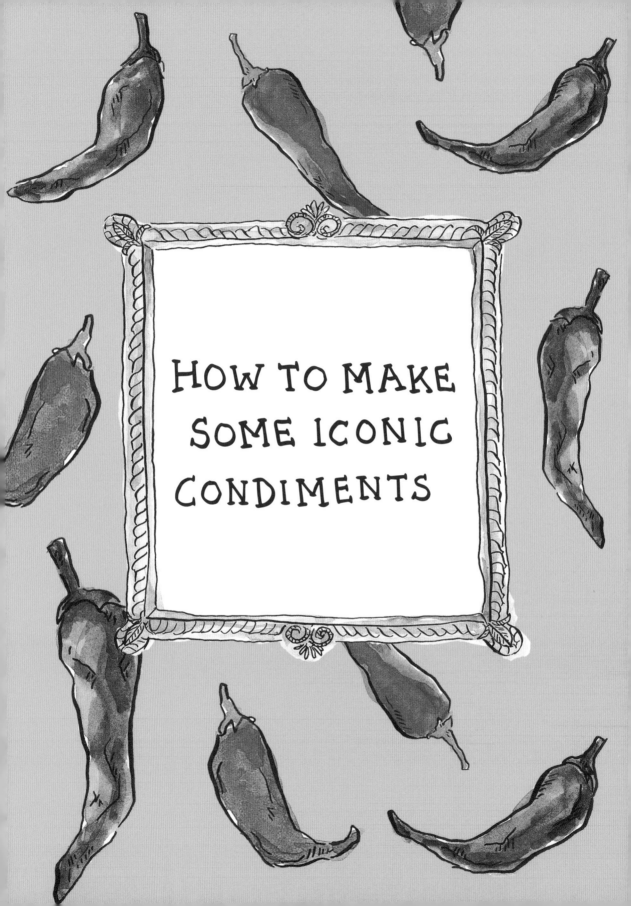

HOW TO MAKE SOME ICONIC CONDIMENTS

Lazy XO Sauce

XO sauce is a Hong Kong invention. Curiously named after XO Cognac,
it actually contains no alcohol – rather, its name simply denotes the prestige of its
luxury ingredients. Making authentic XO sauce is both expensive and incredibly
time-consuming. The dried seafood must be rehydrated overnight, and the ingredients
must be chopped by hand for the perfect mouthfeel.

I've made this sauce properly at restaurants in the past, but at home I don't have
the patience, and I don't want to use my wine money! If we can take its most
important characteristics – spicy, oceanic, smoky and umami-heavy – the
magnificence of XO sauce can be recreated with a little less effort and with
ingredients that are easier to come by.

MAKES 1½ CUPS (375 G)

30 g (1 oz) small dried prawns
    (shrimp)
2 dried Sichuan chillies *(see Notes on
    page 28)*, or other dried chillies
2 teaspoons Shaoxing wine
40 g (1½ oz) prosciutto, cut into
    small pieces
¾ cup (180 ml) vegetable oil
8 cloves garlic, finely chopped
4 French or Asian shallots,
    finely chopped
3 fresh red chillies, finely chopped
Pinch of salt
2 tablespoons oyster sauce
2 tablespoons brown sugar

Place the prawns, dried Sichuan chillies and Shaoxing wine in
a small heatproof bowl. Fill with enough water to just cover.
Microwave on high for 1 minute, then leave to rest on the bench
for 10 minutes to allow the prawns and chillies to rehydrate. Drain
the prawns and chillies, reserving the soaking water.

Place the rehydrated prawns and chillies and the prosciutto into
a food processor and blitz until the mixture resembles breadcrumbs.

Pour the oil into a large saucepan over medium heat. Add the garlic,
shallots and red chillies and gently fry until fragrant. Add the prawn
and prosciutto mixture and continue to fry, stirring continuously,
for 5 minutes or so. Add the reserved soaking water and a pinch
of salt.

Cook over low heat for 25–30 minutes, until the water has
completely evaporated. Add the oyster sauce and brown sugar and
cook for a further 10 minutes. Remove from the heat, then cover
and allow the sauce to infuse in the pan overnight at room
temperature before using.

Stored in an airtight container or jar, this sauce will keep in the
fridge for up to 1 month. Add it to vegetable stir-fries (asparagus
and XO is delicious), or team it with steamed scallops or stir-fried
pippies. It's also great dolloped over fried eggs.

HUNAN SALTED CHILLI

This is a versatile chilli condiment that is excellent to have on hand when you want something brighter and punchier than chilli oil (see page 94). Try to use a mix of long red chillies and small birdseye chillies. The longer ones have a more vegetal flavour and a mid-level heat, whereas birdseye chillies are spicier. Adjust the ratio to suit your taste.

MAKES 1 CUP (250 G)

400 g (14 oz) fresh red chillies
1 head garlic, peeled
¼ cup (60 ml) vodka
1¼ tablespoons brown sugar
2 tablespoons salt

Cut the tops off the chillies and discard. Place the chillies and garlic in a blender or food processor and coarsely blend, keeping the pieces slightly chunky. Transfer to an airtight container and stir in the vodka, sugar and salt. Leave in a sunny spot for 2–3 days, then move to a cooler place for a week.

Stored in an airtight container or jar, this sauce will keep in the fridge for up to 2–3 weeks. Discard if you see any mould or discolouration.

You could combine this chilli with black beans and julienned ginger and spread onto whole fish before steaming it. It also makes an excellent dipping sauce for fried chicken (see pages 155–159) when mixed with some Chinkiang black vinegar, fresh chilli, coriander and soy sauce.

chilli oil

THE COMMON CHINESE NAME FOR CHILLI OIL — HONG YOU (红油),
OR 'RED OIL' — IS A REFERENCE TO ITS ASTONISHINGLY VIBRANT
COLOUR. IN ITS PUREST FORM. CHILLI OIL IS MADE BY POURING
HOT OIL OVER CRUSHED DRIED CHILLIES AND LEAVING THEM TO
INFUSE. I LIKE MINE WITH HEAPS OF SALTY SEDIMENT, AND THIS
RECIPE ENSURES THE MAXIMUM AMOUNT OF 'BITS' AT THE
BOTTOM OF THE JAR.

I'VE DIVIDED THE RECIPE INTO PARTS FOR CLARITY. TRY TO
TRACK DOWN DRIED SICHUAN CHILLIES (SEE NOTES ON PAGE 28).
IF YOU CAN'T, THAT'S FINE, BUT REMEMBER THE HEAT WILL
VARY. THERE ARE A FEW VARIETIES AVAILABLE, RANGING FROM
MODERATE TO VERY SPICY, AND YOUR LOCAL ASIAN GROCER SHOULD
STOCK AT LEAST ONE OF THEM.

MAKES 1½ CUPS (375 ML)

PART 1

40 g (1½ oz) dried Sichuan chillies
(see Notes on page 28), or other
dried chillies
2 tablespoons vegetable oil
1 teaspoon Sichuan peppercorns

PART 2

10 fresh red chillies, topped
3 cloves garlic, peeled
3 cm (1¼ inch) piece ginger, peeled
¼ cup (60 ml) vegetable oil
2 teaspoons salt
2 teaspoons caster (superfine) sugar

PART 3

1 spring onion (scallion),
    white part only
1½ cups (375 ml) vegetable oil
3 cm (1¼ inch) piece ginger,
    skin on, sliced
2 star anise
1 black cardamom pod

PART 1

Use a pair of sharp kitchen scissors to cut the dried chillies into small pieces. Heat the oil in a wok or frying pan and fry the chillies and peppercorns over low heat until they are fragrant and the chillies have turned a deep red. Keep moving the chillies and be extremely careful not to burn them. Allow to cool, then crush using a mortar and pestle. Transfer to a bowl.

PART 2

Place the fresh chillies, garlic and ginger in a food processor and blitz to combine.

Warm the oil in a small saucepan and add the chilli mixture. Fry over low heat until the moisture evaporates, 5–6 minutes. Allow to cool, then stir through the salt and sugar. Combine this mixture with the dried chilli mixture in a heatproof bowl and set aside.

PART 3

Cut the white spring onion into large pieces. Don't cut the pieces too small, or they will cook too quickly and burn.

Pour the oil into a large saucepan that can hold double its volume (as the oil will bubble up) and place over medium heat. Add the spring onion and ginger and fry until golden, then remove from the oil and discard.

Add the star anise and cardamom to the oil and fry over low heat until fragrant. At this point, the oil should be very hot. Pour half the oil over the chilli mixture and stir. Wait 5–6 minutes for the oil to cool slightly, then pour the remaining oil over the chilli mixture.

Once the chilli oil is completely cooled, remove the star anise and cardamom and discard. Cover the oil and leave overnight at room temperature.

The next day, the oil should have turned a dark red colour. Pour into a sterilised airtight container or jar and store in a cool dark place for up to 3 months.

Try this chilli oil on avocado and feta toast, on pasta, or mixed with Chinkiang black vinegar and soy sauce for a classic dumpling dipping sauce.

HOW TO STIR-FRY VEGETABLES

IT PAINS ME TO SEE PACKETS OF VEGETABLES LABELLED AS 'STIR-FRY MIX' AND JARS THAT READ 'STIR-FRY SAUCE' ON SUPERMARKET SHELVES, WHEN THE WORLD OF STIR-FRYING IS ONE FAR BEYOND HAPHAZARD VEGETABLES AND A READY-MADE SAUCE. STIR-FRYING, WHEN DONE CORRECTLY (FEARLESSLY!) OVER HIGH HEAT, NEEDS VERY LITTLE SEASONING, AND CERTAINLY DOESN'T REQUIRE A JAR OF SAUCE. USE THIS TECHNIQUE TO ENHANCE THE BEST VEGETABLES THE SEASON HAS TO OFFER, OR GIVE NEW VIBRANCY TO THE SAD ONES LURKING IN YOUR FRIDGE.

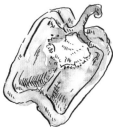

Salt is used in stir-frying the same way it is used in western cooking, to enhance the flavour of the ingredient. Stir-frying vegetables yields spectacular results when done correctly, bringing out a crispness and vibrancy that you won't get from steaming or blanching. The addition of a little salt is all the dish needs to bring out the best from the season's produce.

To work out if a vegetable is appropriate for stir-frying raw, judge how long it takes to cook via other methods, like boiling, roasting or deep-frying. If the vegetable can be cooked quickly, then it can be stir-fried from raw. If it takes longer to cook, it will need to be partly cooked first, before it can be stir-fried.

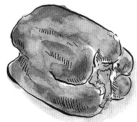

STIR-FRIED LEAFY GREENS

This rapid-fire cooking technique is one of the easiest and most delicious ways to prepare green vegetables. Stir-frying is also the best way to retain nutritional content, and it works well with most vegetables.

SERVES 2 AS A SIDE OR WITH RICE

2 bunches leafy green vegetables such as spinach, gai lan (Chinese broccoli), lettuce or snow pea shoots
2 tablespoons vegetable oil
½ teaspoon salt

Cut the vegetables into 3–4 cm (1¼ –1½ inch) lengths, separating the stems from the leaves.

Heat a wok or frying pan until smoking and add the oil. Add the stems and stir-fry over high heat until bright green and just cooked. Add the leaves and stir-fry until wilted, 20–30 seconds. Season with the salt and serve immediately.

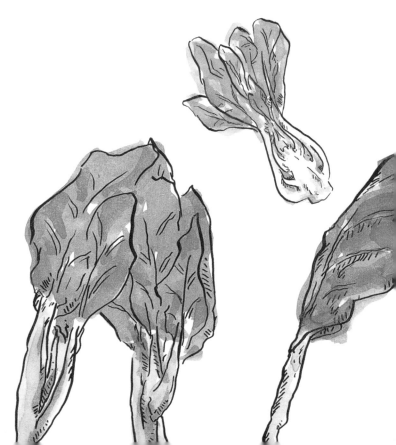

Stir-fried Seasonal Vegetables

It isn't common to find multiple types of vegetables in the one stir-fry dish – they're more likely to be cooked separately using different techniques, and then served as separate dishes. That isn't to say that mixed vegetable dishes don't exist – rather that the vegetables are usually grouped by their type and the time it takes to cook them.

This recipe applies to the broad group of vegetables that are neither leafy greens nor root vegetables. Some common vegetables that stir-fry wonderfully are green peas, celery, flowering cauliflower, broccolini (sprouting broccoli), asparagus and cabbage. We use two cooking techniques here – stir-frying and steaming – to ensure the vegetables are cooked quickly and thoroughly.

**SERVES 2 AS A SIDE
OR WITH RICE**

2 tablespoons vegetable oil
300 g (10½ oz) seasonal vegetables,
   cut into pieces
2 teaspoons sesame oil
½ teaspoon salt

Heat a wok or frying pan until smoking and add the oil. Add the vegetables and stir quickly to coat them in the oil, then stir-fry over high heat until they turn bright green. Add ½ cup (125 ml) water and cover the pan to steam the vegetables for 3–4 minutes, until they are just cooked. Remove the lid, add the sesame oil and salt and continue to stir-fry, uncovered, until all of the water evaporates. Serve immediately.

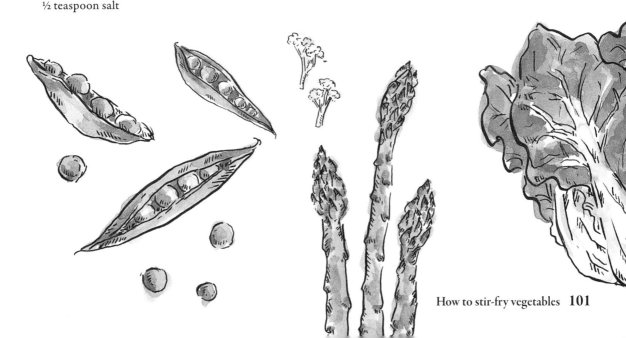

STIR-FRIED SHREDDED POTATO

One of my favourite things about Chinese cuisine is the way potatoes are treated.
They're prepared, cooked and served with rice just like any other vegetable.
The light, crisp texture of the potato in this dish is something to marvel at,
especially if you've only previously tried heavier, western-style potato dishes.
I shred the potatoes with a knife, which is how most Chinese cooks do it, but
a mandolin fitted with the julienne blade or a julienne peeler will work just as well.
It is important that the potatoes retain their al dente quality when cooked.

SERVES 2

2 waxy potatoes, peeled
Iced water
1 teaspoon vegetable oil
2 dried Sichuan chillies *(see Notes on page 28)*, or other dried chillies
1 clove garlic, minced
¼ green capsicum (pepper), thinly sliced
Salt, to taste
2 teaspoons sesame oil
Steamed rice, to serve

Shred the potatoes into a bowl of iced water. Make sure the potatoes are fully submerged and rub them in the water to remove the starch from their surface. This process ensures they retain a crisp texture once fried. Soak the potatoes in the water for 30 minutes, then drain them well just before cooking.

Heat a wok or frying pan over medium–high heat and add the oil. Stir-fry the dried chillies until they just begin to darken. Reduce the heat, add the garlic and fry for 10–20 seconds until fragrant.

Increase the heat to high and add the shredded potatoes, sliced capsicum and 1 tablespoon water. Stir-fry until the potatoes are just cooked but still crisp. Season with salt, remove from the heat and add the sesame oil. Serve the potatoes with steamed rice.

FRIED CORN WITH SPICED SALT

WHENEVER I WRITE THE WORDS 'DEEP-FRY' IN A RECIPE, I KNOW THAT SOME PEOPLE WILL IMMEDIATELY STOP READING. I OFTEN DEEP-FRY AT HOME BECAUSE, FOR CERTAIN DISHES, YOU SIMPLY CAN'T ACHIEVE THE SAME TEXTURE WITHOUT IT. I DEEP-FRY IN A WOK WHICH, THANKS TO ITS CURVED EDGES, USES SIGNIFICANTLY LESS OIL THAN A SAUCEPAN. I ALSO RETAIN THE OIL BY STRAINING IT INTO A SMALL METAL CONTAINER, USING IT SLOWLY OVER THE COURSE OF A WEEK OR TWO.

FUNNILY ENOUGH, THE HIGH TEMPERATURE AND THE SHORT TIME THE INGREDIENTS SPEND IN THE OIL DURING DEEP-FRYING MEANS THAT THEY ACTUALLY ABSORB VERY LITTLE OIL. DURING SHALLOW-FRYING, INGREDIENTS CAN END UP RATHER GREASY BY SUCKING UP A LOT OF THE OIL IN THE PAN; DEFINITELY SOMETHING TO CONSIDER WHEN CHASING A 'HEALTHIER' OPTION.

WHILE FRESH CORN IS MAGNIFICENT WHEN IN SEASON, YOU CAN ALSO USE FROZEN CORN FOR THIS RECIPE. FROZEN CORN KERNELS ARE ALREADY COOKED AND DON'T NEED TO GO THROUGH THE BLANCHING PROCESS. IF YOU'RE USING FROZEN CORN, ENSURE IT IS THOROUGHLY DEFROSTED AND DRY, THEN SKIP THE FIRST STEP.

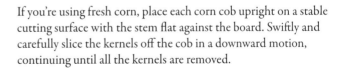

SERVES 4

3 corn cobs or 1⅔ cups (250 g)
    defrosted corn kernels
Iced water
2 cups (500 ml) vegetable oil,
    plus 2 teaspoons extra
About ½ cup (60 g) cornflour
    (cornstarch)
6 dried Sichuan chillies *(see Notes on*
    page 28), or other dried chillies
2 cm (¾ inch) piece ginger, minced
2 cloves garlic, minced
2 spring onions (scallions), sliced,
    green and white parts kept separate

SPICED SALT
1 teaspoon salt
1 teaspoon five spice powder
½ teaspoon caster (superfine) sugar
½ teaspoon ground white pepper

If you're using fresh corn, place each corn cob upright on a stable cutting surface with the stem flat against the board. Swiftly and carefully slice the kernels off the cob in a downward motion, continuing until all the kernels are removed.

Blanch the corn kernels in a large saucepan of boiling water. The corn is cooked when the kernels begin to float. Drain and refresh in iced water. When completely cold, drain corn thoroughly and set aside.

To make the spiced salt, mix all of the ingredients to combine. Set aside.

Heat the vegetable oil in a heavy-based wok or frying pan to 170°C (325°F) using a food thermometer to check the temperature. Toss the blanched or defrosted corn kernels and cornflour together in a bowl, ensuring the individual kernels are well coated and separated from each other. Add more cornflour if necessary.

Carefully lower the floured corn into the hot oil and deep-fry for 30 seconds, until the kernels crisp up. Remove from the oil and drain on paper towel. Fry the corn once more, this time for 10–15 seconds, to ensure it stays crispy. Transfer to paper towel to absorb any excess oil, then set aside.

Heat the extra vegetable oil in a separate wok or frying pan and add the dried Sichuan chillies. Fry until they begin to turn dark red, then add the ginger, garlic and sliced white spring onion. Fry over medium heat until aromatic, taking care not to burn the garlic. As soon as everything starts to smell delicious, add the crisped corn kernels and toss to combine, then remove from the heat.

Sprinkle some of the spiced salt over the corn, along with the sliced green spring onion. Taste for seasoning and add more spiced salt, if necessary, before serving. Remember – you can always add more, but you can't remove the salt once it's added, so start small.

FRIED CORN
WITH SPICED
SALT

SEE PAGE 104

SICHUAN
TIGER-SKIN
PEPPERS

SEE PAGE 108

SICHUAN TIGER-SKIN PEPPERS

'TIGER-SKIN' (虎皮尖椒) REFERS TO THE SCORCHED STRIPE MARKS ON THE SKIN OF THE PEPPERS FROM 'DRY' FRYING THEM. THE BLISTERING TURNS THE PEPPERS SOFT AND SWEET, WHICH IS DELICIOUS IN A GARLICKY SWEET AND SOUR SAUCE. THE SAUCE IS ALSO PERFECT FOR BALANCING ANY RESIDUAL SPICINESS FROM THE PEPPERS.

YOU'LL WANT TO SOURCE 'EATING PEPPERS' WITH A MILD TO MEDIUM HEAT, SUCH AS ITALIAN FRYING PEPPERS, PADRÓN OR SHISHITO PEPPERS. IT IS UNWISE TO TRY AND COOK THIS DISH WITH JALAPEÑOS OR ANY OTHER CHILLIES USED FOR THEIR HEAT, AS THIS IS MEANT TO BE EATEN AS A DISH, NOT A CONDIMENT.

IF YOU ARE UNABLE TO SOURCE APPROPRIATE 'EATING PEPPERS', YOU CAN USE SOME VARIETIES OF CAPSICUM OR LONG TURKISH PEPPERS. AT THE TIME OF WRITING, NEITHER PADRÓN NOR SHISHITO PEPPERS WERE IN SEASON, SO I USED A COMBINATION OF BANANA PEPPERS AND BABY CAPSICUMS.

SERVES 4

2 tablespoons light soy sauce
½ teaspoon caster (superfine) sugar
1 tablespoon Chinkiang black vinegar
¼ teaspoon salt
¼ cup (60 ml) vegetable oil
10 'eating peppers' (padrón peppers,
    shishito peppers, banana peppers,
    baby capsicum or similar),
    deseeded and halved
4 cloves garlic, minced
Steamed rice, to serve

Combine the soy sauce, sugar, Chinkiang vinegar and salt in a bowl and set aside.

Heat a wok or frying pan until smoking and add 2 tablespoons oil. Swirl the oil around to coat the surface, then add the peppers. Spread the peppers around so that they are all in contact with the hot surface and cook over medium heat, turning occasionally, until the skins are blistered and starting to wrinkle.

When the peppers are ready, move them to one side of the wok and add the remaining oil. Fry the garlic over medium heat until aromatic, then add the soy sauce mixture and simmer until it begins to thicken. Push the peppers back into the middle of the pan and toss to coat them in the sauce.

This dish can be eaten hot with steamed rice, but it is also delicious cold.

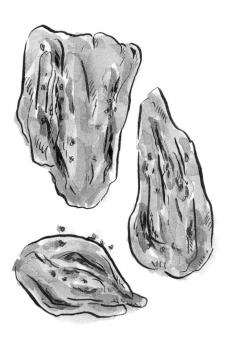

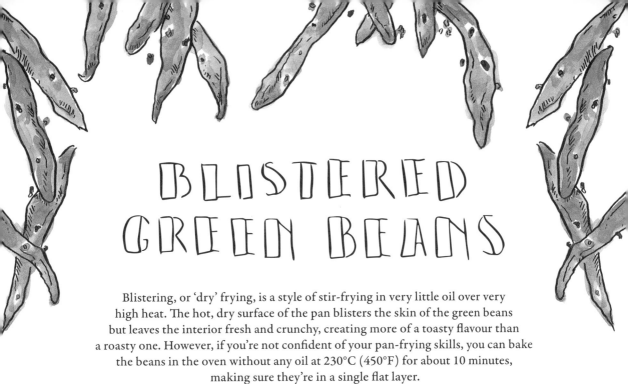

BLISTERED GREEN BEANS

Blistering, or 'dry' frying, is a style of stir-frying in very little oil over very high heat. The hot, dry surface of the pan blisters the skin of the green beans but leaves the interior fresh and crunchy, creating more of a toasty flavour than a roasty one. However, if you're not confident of your pan-frying skills, you can bake the beans in the oven without any oil at 230°C (450°F) for about 10 minutes, making sure they're in a single flat layer.

SERVES 4

2 teaspoons vegetable oil
400 g (14 oz) green beans, cut into
   5 cm (2 inch) lengths
6 dried Sichuan chillies *(see Notes on page 28)*, or other dried chillies
1 teaspoon Sichuan peppercorns
2 cm (¾ inch) piece ginger, minced
3 cloves garlic, minced
2 spring onions (scallions), white part
   only, cut into 2 cm (¾ inch) lengths
Salt, to taste
Sesame oil and steamed rice, to serve

Heat 1 teaspoon vegetable oil in a wok or frying pan until smoking. Add the green beans and stir-fry over high heat until the skins are wrinkly but the beans are still bright green. Remove green beans and set aside.

Heat the remaining vegetable oil until smoking. Reduce the heat to low and add the dried Sichuan chillies and peppercorns. Stir-fry until fragrant, taking care not to burn the chillies. Add the ginger, garlic and white spring onion and stir-fry until fragrant.

Return the green beans to the wok and season with salt. Finish with a small splash of sesame oil and serve with steamed rice.

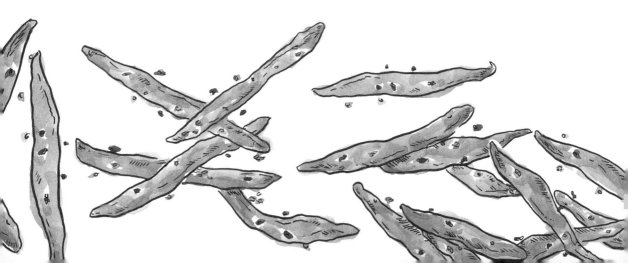

THREE EARTHLY TREASURES

This is a really lovely homestyle Northern Chinese dish. It's a rustic stir-fry of crisp fried potato, soft eggplant and crunchy capsicum (pepper), tossed through a fragrant garlic sauce, with each vegetable providing a different texture.

We use a technique here called 'head and tail garlic' (头尾蒜), where minced garlic is added at the beginning and end of the cooking process. It provides incredible depth to the dish, offering both a warm, caramelised flavour and that exquisite fragrance of just-cooked garlic.

SERVES 4

1 large eggplant (aubergine),
    cut into bite-size pieces
1 teaspoon salt
½ cup (60 g) cornflour (cornstarch)
1 cup (250 ml) vegetable oil
1 floury potato, peeled, halved
    lengthways and cut into
    1 cm (½ inch) slices
1 green capsicum (pepper),
    cut into bite-size pieces
4 cloves garlic, minced

SAUCE
2 tablespoons light soy sauce
½ teaspoon dark soy sauce
¼ teaspoon caster (superfine) sugar
1 teaspoon cornflour (cornstarch)

Submerge the eggplant in water with the salt. Allow it to soak for 15 minutes, then drain thoroughly and pat dry with paper towel. Toss the eggplant and cornflour together until coated and set aside.

Heat the oil in a wok or frying pan until smoking and fry the potato slices until they are a dark golden colour and wrinkled. Drain and set aside.

In the same oil, fry the floured eggplant pieces until tender, then drain and set aside.

Briefly fry the capsicum until it turns bright green. Remove from the oil and set aside with the other vegetables.

Mix all of the ingredients for the sauce together with 2 tablespoons water in a small bowl to combine. Remove all but 1 tablespoon of oil from the pan. Add half the garlic and fry until aromatic, then add the sauce. Bring to the boil, then return the vegetables to the wok and toss to coat them in the sauce. Add the remaining garlic, fry for 1 minute over high heat and serve.

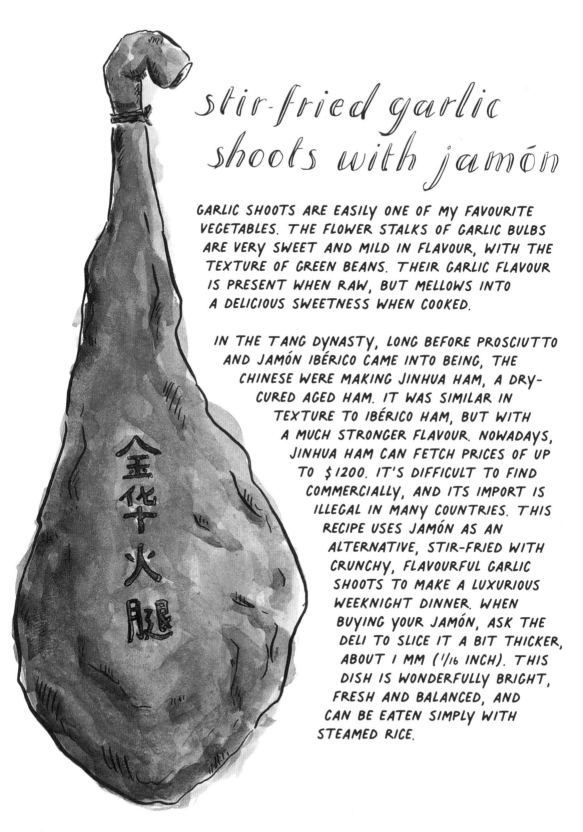

stir-fried garlic shoots with jamón

GARLIC SHOOTS ARE EASILY ONE OF MY FAVOURITE VEGETABLES. THE FLOWER STALKS OF GARLIC BULBS ARE VERY SWEET AND MILD IN FLAVOUR, WITH THE TEXTURE OF GREEN BEANS. THEIR GARLIC FLAVOUR IS PRESENT WHEN RAW, BUT MELLOWS INTO A DELICIOUS SWEETNESS WHEN COOKED.

IN THE TANG DYNASTY, LONG BEFORE PROSCIUTTO AND JAMÓN IBÉRICO CAME INTO BEING, THE CHINESE WERE MAKING JINHUA HAM, A DRY-CURED AGED HAM. IT WAS SIMILAR IN TEXTURE TO IBÉRICO HAM, BUT WITH A MUCH STRONGER FLAVOUR. NOWADAYS, JINHUA HAM CAN FETCH PRICES OF UP TO $1200. IT'S DIFFICULT TO FIND COMMERCIALLY, AND ITS IMPORT IS ILLEGAL IN MANY COUNTRIES. THIS RECIPE USES JAMÓN AS AN ALTERNATIVE, STIR-FRIED WITH CRUNCHY, FLAVOURFUL GARLIC SHOOTS TO MAKE A LUXURIOUS WEEKNIGHT DINNER. WHEN BUYING YOUR JAMÓN, ASK THE DELI TO SLICE IT A BIT THICKER, ABOUT 1 MM (1/16 INCH). THIS DISH IS WONDERFULLY BRIGHT, FRESH AND BALANCED, AND CAN BE EATEN SIMPLY WITH STEAMED RICE.

SERVES 2

1 bunch garlic shoots *(see Note)*
¼ cup (60 ml) vegetable oil
2 slices jamón, cut into thick strips
½ teaspoon salt
½ teaspoon sesame oil

Prepare the garlic shoots by cutting 1 cm (½ inch) off the ends, as you would trim asparagus. If they seem fibrous, you may need to cut off more. Slice the garlic shoots into 4 cm (1½ inch) pieces and set aside.

Heat the vegetable oil in a wok or frying pan over high heat until smoking. Add the jamón and fry until crisp. Add the garlic shoots and stir-fry over medium–high heat until just tender. Season with the salt and toss to combine. Remove from the heat, add the sesame oil and toss through the garlic shoots. Transfer to a plate and serve.

NOTE
Garlic shoots are available at most Asian grocers and some farmers' markets.

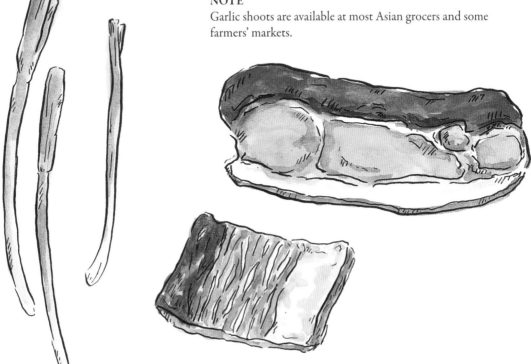

STIR-FRIED
GARLIC SHOOTS
WITH JAMÓN
SEE PAGE 114

YUNNAN
MASHED
POTATO
SEE PAGE 118

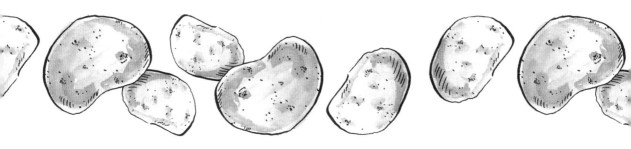

Yunnan Mashed Potato

IN YUNNAN, MASHED POTATO (老奶洋芋) IS APPARENTLY MORE POPULAR AMONG TOURISTS THAN LOCALS. I'VE ALREADY WRITTEN ABOUT HOW MUCH I LOVE CHINESE POTATO DISHES, AND THIS DISH IS ANOTHER SHINING EXAMPLE. IT REALLY IS JUST OLD-FAITHFUL MASHED POTATO, BUT STIR-FRIED WITH HEADY SPICES AND PICKLED VEGETABLES. IT'S COMFORT FOOD, BUT NOT AS YOU KNOW IT. IF I SAW THIS ON A MENU IN AN UNFAMILIAR CITY, I WOULD DEFINITELY POINT TO THE PICTURE AND ORDER IT.

THIS RECIPE IS MADE EXTRA-DELICIOUS BY THE ADDITION OF SUAN CAI (酸腌菜), WHICH ARE PICKLED MUSTARD GREENS. THE SPICY YUNNAN VERSION OF SUAN CAI CAN BE FOUND IN VACUUM-SEALED PACKS AT WELL-STOCKED ASIAN GROCERS. IF YOUR LOCAL ASIAN GROCER DOESN'T HAVE NICHE REGIONAL CHINESE PICKLES, SOUTHEAST ASIANS ALSO HAPPEN TO EAT PICKLED MUSTARD GREENS. THEY KNOW THEM AS KIAM CHAI OR HUM CHOY, AND THESE ARE ALSO WIDELY AVAILABLE AT ASIAN GROCERS. IF YOU'RE REALLY STRUGGLING TO FIND EITHER, YOU CAN OMIT THEM COMPLETELY.

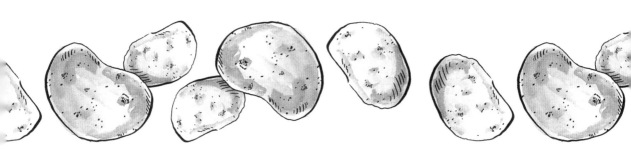

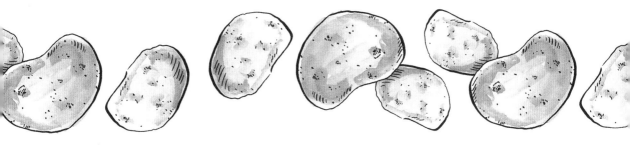

SERVES 4

500 g (1 lb 2 oz) starchy potatoes,
    peeled and cut into small pieces
2 tablespoons vegetable oil
4 cloves garlic, minced
2 spring onions (scallions), sliced,
    green and white parts kept separate
2 tablespoons *suan cai* (pickled
    mustard greens), minced
1 teaspoon Sichuan or regular
    chilli powder *(see Notes on page 38)*
½ teaspoon salt
1 tablespoon chilli oil (see page 94,
    or use Lao Gan Ma chilli oil),
    to serve

Boil the potatoes in a large saucepan of boiling water until tender. Drain and set aside, reserving 2 tablespoons of the starchy cooking water.

Heat 1 tablespoon of the vegetable oil in a wok or non-stick frying pan. Add the garlic and stir-fry over high heat until fragrant. Add the sliced white spring onion and fry for a few seconds, then add the *suan cai* and fry briefly. Add the chilli powder and fry until fragrant.

Reduce the heat to medium and add the cooked potatoes and reserved starchy cooking water. Using a spatula, start crushing the potatoes and frying them simultaneously. You want a bit of textural contrast, so don't worry too much about mashing the potatoes smoothly. Slowly turn the heat back up to medium–high.

Add the remaining vegetable oil to the wok and continue to fry the potatoes for 2–3 minutes. The additional oil is to make sure the wok's surface remains non-stick and to prevent the potatoes from becoming a gluey mess. Add the salt and sliced green spring onion. Stir for 10–15 seconds, then taste and add more salt if necessary. Transfer to a plate in a nice mound and drizzle with chilli oil.

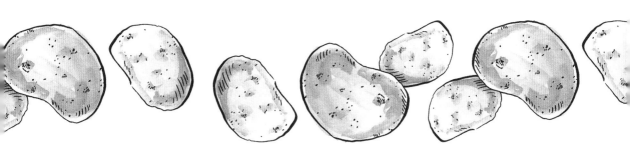

PART TWO

The Rebellion:
How to
Disappoint
Your Parents

THERE AND BACK AGAIN

JO： While listening to an episode of the *Asian Not Asian* podcast titled 'Falling off the Rainbow Road', I was struck by an analogy used to describe the way the children of Asian immigrants are raised. Loosely paraphrasing, there is apparently a playbook for how their childhood is supposed to go: piano or violin lessons, tennis lessons, maths tuition, volunteering (enough to go on the high-school transcript), and then onto an 'acceptable' degree such as medicine, law or engineering. And so these kids are on what feels like the rainbow road in *Mario Kart*, suspended in space while they try to follow this playbook, but there's no safety net if they fall off the edge.

For the longest time, I found myself on this rainbow road. My path had all the hallmarks of the traditional 'Asian excellence' route: piano, Kumon maths tutoring, Chinese school and a restricted social life. But to summarise the five years following my high-school graduation, a failure to get into medicine resulted in a knee-jerk decision to study law, leading to five years of confusion, academic failure, self-loathing and isolation.

Enter hospitality.

It was at the height of season two of *MasterChef Australia*, before the TV-born food careers of all those reality cooking show contestants had been established. And yet, these people were giving up stable jobs and hard-won careers to take a chance on something they were passionate about. I remember crying while studying for an exam one night, wishing I could love anything as much as these people loved food. Despite not really having any previous interest in food or hospitality, I thought that perhaps this industry could be for me. It goes to show you just how lost I was, trying on other people's dreams to see if they fit.

I still remember the Sunday afternoon in October when I stumbled upon a job ad for Melbourne's Vue de Monde restaurant group. With no idea about its reputation, and no concept of how inexperienced I was, I wrote an enthusiastic cover letter detailing my four months of experience working as a waiter in a suburban cafe. By some miracle, my application progressed to the interview stage, which led to a trial shift (during which I was so nervous about not dropping anything that I walked straight into a glass door), and that resulted in a job offer. Perhaps my naivety and openness to learning actually helped me.

My cultural upbringing was one of austerity and sacrifice – we hardly ever ate out, and never at expensive restaurants. I watched my mother refrain from buying new clothes for six years, so she could put me through private school.

But here, I had entered a new world, one grounded in the physical pleasures of eating and drinking. A world of appetites and fulfilling them: intoxicating stuff.

My parents struggled to understand the appeal of my career change. To them, it seemed inconceivable that they worked so hard at those early dishwashing jobs to give me a good education, only for me to dive willingly into that same environment, albeit in a different role. But they had also witnessed my five years of misery during my university degree, so my renewed motivation for any aspect of life came as a welcome relief.

In my new restaurant job, I was being exposed to all kinds of people and developing an all-new skill set. Everything seemed based on tactile, earthly gratification. What could I try? What would I enjoy at this very moment? We were constantly chasing the ephemeral – that perfectly balanced bite of food, that sip of wine drunk at just the right time, that ideal meal service where everything ran perfectly. It was heady, addictive stuff. Our working hours were so unsociable that you often lost connection with those in your life who weren't in the industry. Instead, you formed 'found families' with your colleagues, celebrated orphan Christmases, and developed the kind of bonds that could only be forged at 4am, watching the first rays of the sunrise after one too many knock-off drinks.

After a stint at Heston Blumenthal's The Fat Duck, during their six-month Melbourne pop-up, I was asked to move back to the UK with them. It was there that I was exposed to the European level of fine dining. I shook hands with a member of the royal family, I worked at a function on the ski slopes of Mont Blanc, and I dined my way around New York City like royalty. I felt like a valued employee – my opinions were taken seriously and, most special of all, my artistic abilities were nurtured and encouraged.

When it came time to leave at the conclusion of my working visa, I felt a return of uncertainty and the same feeling of being lost that had launched my hospitality career – it had been quietly nagging at me for a while.

As someone who had always been bookish and introverted, I found the challenge of playing someone who was cheerful and charismatic a bit of a thrill at first. Maybe that's why I relished the idea of working so much: the less time I had to myself, the better. But a charade like that can't last forever.

I really loved hospitality – I loved it the way you love something that saves your life. The years since then have been a difficult process of reconciling the extremes of what felt like soulless study in pursuit of a white-collar job, and the bright, burning passion I felt while working in an all-consuming industry.

In a way, perhaps my current path of artistic pursuits was there all along. From the time a fellow student in one of my law lectures walked past me while I was drawing in my notebook and commented, *'You shouldn't be here, you should be doing that instead'.* Or when I took my first tentative steps towards working in a restaurant where my drawing skills would later be recognised and encouraged. What I once saw as a detour from the main road, perhaps led me to the path I should have taken all along.

And just because something doesn't last forever, that doesn't make it any less important.

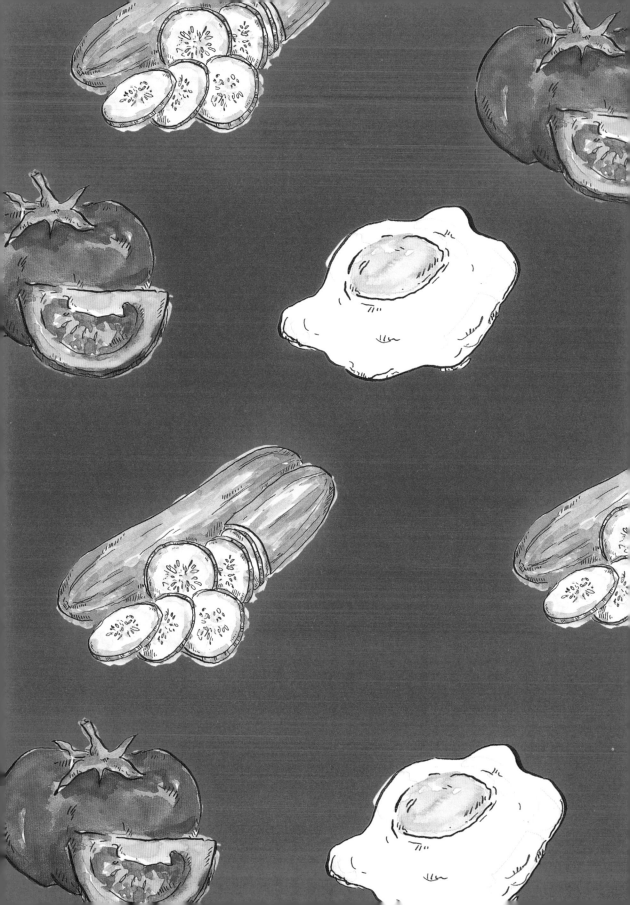

THE SOLO DINER

AN ODE TO EGGS

JO： I love eggs. I've often considered a pure vegan diet, save for giving up these cholesterol-rich delights. I've had nightmares about what a life of being allergic to eggs would be like. For me, they are nature's true superfood, suitable for all manner of savoury and sweet dishes. They possess great flavour of their own, but also act as a kind of magic binding agent to unite disparate elements. And they make the perfect cost-effective ingredient when preparing food for one person.

My love of eggs started young, with the classic dish of stir-fried tomato and egg (番茄炒蛋; see page 135). It's a tasty, easy meal to make for children. During my 'vegetables are not for me' phase, stir-fried tomato was my only source of dietary fibre. My parents also strongly believed in the school of thought that eggs were brain food, so they encouraged my egg consumption.

One of the most horrifying things I've ever revealed about myself to people is how much I love a really, really hard-boiled egg, the kind where the yolk turns dark grey at the edges. I will happily peel and eat these like apples – no condiments needed. But yes, I will also slather an egg in its tangy, smoother condiment cousin: mayonnaise.

Fret not, though, for Rosheen has chosen some delicious egg recipes that don't involve boiling your yolks into a powder, or squeezing mayonnaise straight into your mouth ...

'OH, IT'S SO CUTE. SHE SOMETIMES TAKES A LITTLE PACK OF MAYONNAISE, AND SHE'LL SQUIRT IT IN HER MOUTH ALL OVER, AND THEN SHE'LL TAKE AN EGG AND KIND OF ... MMMMM! SHE CALLS IT A 'MAYONEGG'.'
- GEORGE MICHAEL, ARRESTED DEVELOPMENT

steamed savoury egg custard two ways

This savoury egg custard, or egg tofu, is a fantastic one-person dish. The concept is very simple: whisk an egg with warm chicken stock and a touch of seasoning and cook it very gently. The cooked custard can be dressed simply with a little more soy sauce and sesame oil, or topped with seafood and steamed for a further few minutes. Either way, it's one of life's simplest pleasures.

SERVES 1

1 egg
½ cup (125 ml) warm stock
    (see page 51), or use a good-quality
    store-bought stock
1 teaspoon light soy sauce

Thoroughly whisk the egg, warm stock and soy sauce together and then drain into a small heatproof bowl.

TO COOK IN THE MICROWAVE
Cover with a lid and microwave at 50 per cent power for 2 minutes. Check the consistency after 2 minutes and wipe away any water droplets that appear on the lid. From here, microwave in 30-second increments at 50 per cent power until the custard is just set.

TO STEAM
Cover the bowl tightly with plastic wrap and pierce holes in the plastic to allow steam to escape. Place in a bamboo steamer and steam over a gentle heat for 10–12 minutes, or until just set.

NOTE
The suggested microwave times above are for an 1100-watt microwave.

CHIFFON OMELETTE

THEY SAY THE KEY TO A PERFECT OMELETTE IS THE RIGHT TECHNIQUE AND A LOT OF PATIENCE. IF WE'RE TALKING ABOUT THE FRENCH OMELETTE, THAT IS ABSOLUTELY RIGHT. BY THIS DEFINITION, A PERFECT OMELETTE HAS A PALE AND EVEN YELLOW COLOUR, WITH NO SIGNS OF CARAMELISATION. WHILE THE SURFACE OF THE OMELETTE IS PERFECTLY SET, THE CENTRE IS JUST UNDERDONE, GIVING WAY TO A CUSTARDY INTERIOR WHEN SLICED OPEN. PERFECTION, AS THEY SAY.

THE MASALA OMELETTES, FRIED OYSTER OMELETTES AND GREEN BEAN OMELETTES OF MY CHILDHOOD ALL BEG TO DIFFER. CRISP, FLUFFY AND GOLDEN — A RESULT OF PLENTY OF OIL AND PLENTY OF HEAT — THE ASIAN APPROACH TO OMELETTES CHAMPIONS ALL OF THE CHARACTERISTICS THE WESTERN WORLD CONDEMNS.

THIS OMELETTE RECIPE IS A HYBRID OF THE THAI KHAI JIAO AND EGG FOO YOUNG (芙蓉蛋). EGGS ARE WHISKED THOROUGHLY, COMBINED WITH FILLINGS OF YOUR CHOICE AND FRIED IN HOT OIL TO CREATE GOLDEN CLOUDS.

YOU CAN INTRODUCE AS MANY OR AS FEW FILLINGS AS YOU LIKE — JUST ENSURE THAT THEY ARE SLICED THINLY ENOUGH TO COOK QUICKLY, OR ARE ALREADY COOKED. I HAVE WRITTEN AS MANY SUGGESTIONS FOR FILLINGS AS I CAN THINK OF, BUT FEEL FREE TO IMPROVISE. I PARTICULARLY LIKE THE VERSION WITH CRAB AND SPRING ONION (SCALLION).

MAKES 1 TO SHARE BETWEEN 2

4 eggs
1 teaspoon salt
¼ teaspoon ground white pepper
1 tablespoon cornflour (cornstarch)
    blended with 1 tablespoon water
2 spring onions (scallions), white part
    cut into 3 cm (1¼ inch) lengths,
    green part thinly sliced
50 g (1¾ oz) shredded *char siu*
    (Cantonese barbecued pork),
    ham or cooked chicken
50 g (1¾ oz) cooked crab meat or
    cooked prawns (shrimp)
50–60 g (1¾ oz–2¼ oz) julienned
    fresh shiitake mushrooms,
    bamboo shoots, carrots,
    bean sprouts or brown onion
1 cup (250 ml) vegetable oil
Steamed rice, to serve

Whisk the eggs, salt, white pepper and cornflour slurry together thoroughly. Ensure there are no strands of egg white remaining and that the mixture is well combined. Add the white spring onion, cooked meat and seafood, and the julienned vegetables, then stir to combine with the egg mixture. Set aside.

Heat the vegetable oil in a wok or frying pan until smoking and pour the egg mixture in. It will puff up as soon as it hits the hot oil.

Allow the omelette to cook for 10 seconds, then tilt the pan to allow the egg mixture to run from the centre of the omelette into the oil. Repeat the process until the omelette is fluffy, evenly cooked and beginning to crisp around the edges. It should resemble a soft yellow cloud. Lift the omelette gently with your spatula and flip it. Cook for 10 seconds on the other side.

Remove the omelette from the wok and drain on paper towel to absorb the excess oil. Serve with sliced green spring onion and steamed rice.

CHIFFON
OMELETTE
SEE PAGE 130

STIR-FRIED TOMATO & EGG

When tomatoes first arrived in China, they were initially named 'foreign eggplants' and met with thinly veiled scepticism. They eventually made their way into someone's wok, along with scrambled eggs and spring onion (scallion), and so stir-fried tomato and egg (蕃茄炒蛋) found its way into many homes in China.

Eating tender, fluffy eggs with umami-laden tomato isn't too different from eating scrambled eggs with tomato sauce (ketchup) in the morning. This dish may not seem particularly Asian, but it's as traditional as it gets.

SERVES 2

2 large eggs
½ teaspoon salt, plus extra to taste
¼ teaspoon ground white pepper
2 tablespoons vegetable oil
1 very ripe tomato,
    cut into 8 wedges
1 spring onion (scallion), cut into
    3 cm (1¼ inch) lengths
¼ teaspoon caster (superfine) sugar
Sesame oil and steamed rice,
    to serve

Crack the eggs into a bowl and season with the salt and white pepper. Whisk until well combined and lightly frothy.

Heat 1 tablespoon vegetable oil in a wok over medium–high heat until smoking. Turn the heat off and add the egg mixture. Cook for 20 seconds without stirring, then turn the heat back to medium–high. Gently scramble the eggs and transfer to a plate. The eggs should still be very soft.

Wipe out the wok and heat the remaining vegetable oil over medium–high heat. Add the tomato wedges and spring onion and fry until the tomatoes start to soften, pressing down gently on each wedge with the back of a spoon to help it along. Don't crush the tomatoes completely, as you want some nice large pieces to remain.

Once the tomatoes begin to release some of their juices, return the cooked eggs to the pan and season with extra salt and the sugar. Taste and adjust the seasoning if necessary. Remove from the heat and drizzle with a little sesame oil. Serve piping hot with rice.

CREAMY TOFU NOODLES WITH SOY-VINEGAR DRESSING

Tofu is so terribly misunderstood in the western world. I will admit that it doesn't have much going on taste-wise, but it is such an excellent vehicle for other flavours. Whether it's delicate, silky curds in a simple dressing, or crispy, golden puffs in a stir-fry, tofu is easily one of my favourite ingredients.

I ate tofu with soy sauce and chilli every single day after I got my wisdom teeth removed, and this dish fondly reminds me of that time. Here, tofu is transformed into a creamy sauce, wrapping the noodles in a velvety blanket, while the zingy dressing perks up your tastebuds.

SERVES 1

150 g (5½ oz) fresh or dried
    thin wheat noodles
300 g (10½ oz) firm tofu
¼ teaspoon salt
¼ teaspoon caster (superfine) sugar

SOY-VINEGAR DRESSING
1 tablespoon light soy sauce
1 teaspoon Chinkiang black vinegar
1 teaspoon grated ginger
1 teaspoon grated garlic
1 red chilli, finely chopped
1 green chilli, finely chopped
1 spring onion (scallion),
    finely chopped
4 coriander (cilantro) sprigs,
    finely chopped
2 teaspoons sesame seeds

Bring a large saucepan of water to the boil and cook the noodles according to the packet instructions. Drain thoroughly and set aside.

Drain the tofu, then break it into pieces. Place the tofu in a blender or food processor with the salt, sugar and 1 tablespoon water and blend until completely smooth.

Toss the drained noodles through the blended tofu until the noodles are well coated.

To make the soy-vinegar dressing, combine all of the ingredients together with 1 tablespoon water in a small bowl. Spoon the dressing over the noodles, mix thoroughly and serve immediately.

Smashed Cucumber Salad

It's not often you come across a dish that is as much fun to prepare as it is to eat.
Smacking the cucumber with the back of a knife or cleaver, or even a hammer,
creates lovely nooks and crevices for the dressing to find its way into,
resulting in a punchy, refreshing dish for those swelteringly hot days.

SERVES 1

1 Lebanese (short) cucumber
½ teaspoon salt
Coriander (cilantro) leaves, to serve

DRESSING
1 tablespoon light soy sauce
1 tablespoon sesame oil
1 tablespoon chilli oil (see page 94,
    or use Lao Gan Mao chilli oil)
1 tablespoon Chinkiang black vinegar
3 cloves garlic, grated
1 teaspoon caster (superfine) sugar

Top and tail the cucumber and halve it lengthways. Use the blunt edge of a knife or cleaver to smash it into bite-size pieces. Sprinkle with the salt and allow to stand for 10 minutes to draw out the excess moisture. Rinse off the salt and drain the cucumber in a colander, then pat it dry with paper towel.

To make the dressing, mix all the ingredients to combine. Toss the cucumber through the dressing to coat, top with coriander leaves and serve.

NOTE
If chilli oil isn't your thing, you can make a milder version of this salad. Heat 1 tablespoon vegetable oil until smoking and pour it over the salad instead of the chilli oil, along with the dressing. The flavour of cooked oil (熟油) is a common and welcome addition to fresh garnishes and condiments in Chinese cuisine.

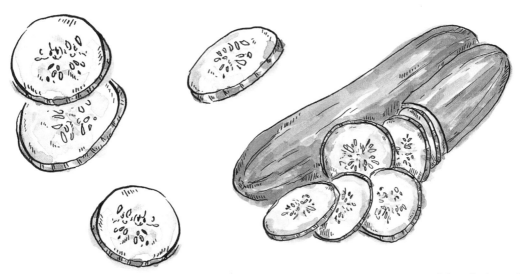

BURNT SPRING ONION OIL NOODLES

Spring onion oil noodles (葱油拌面) are deceptively moreish, yet quick and easy. Somehow, frying spring onion (scallion) in plenty of oil until almost burnt, and then adding a touch of soy and vinegar, creates a deeply umami savouriness. It's not a bad idea to make a large batch of the spring onion oil – stored in an airtight jar, it will keep for up to 1 month in the fridge, and then it's a simple matter of tossing it through cooked noodles for a fast, satisfying meal.

SERVES 1

⅓ cup (80 ml) vegetable oil
4 spring onions (scallions), cut into
    6 cm (2½ inch) lengths
2 tablespoons light soy sauce
¼ teaspoon dark soy sauce
2 teaspoons Chinkiang black vinegar
150 g (5½ oz) fresh or dried noodles
    of your choice

Bring a large saucepan of water to the boil. Meanwhile, heat the oil in a wok or frying pan until smoking and add the spring onion. Stir-fry until fragrant and a deep golden-brown, almost burnt. Transfer the oil and spring onion to a bowl and set aside.

Combine the soy sauces and Chinkiang vinegar together in a large bowl. Cook the noodles in the boiling water according to the packet instructions. Drain the noodles and transfer to the bowl with the soy sauce mixture. Pour the reserved oil and caramelised spring onion over the top and mix thoroughly before eating.

MICROWAVE CHEONG FUN

This recipe was inspired by one I saw on 'Subtle Asian Traits', a Facebook page dedicated to sharing jokes and memes about the Asian experience in the west. My version is possibly not as delicate as traditional steamed rice noodle rolls, but it's pretty darn close. If you don't have a steamer at home but you do have a microwave, you can definitely still make this yum cha favourite. A word to the wise – don't try to make *cheong fun* for a crowd. It will take forever, and you will definitely lose interest by the time you're four rolls in.

SERVES 1

1¼ cups (200 g) rice flour
1 tablespoon sesame oil
1 tablespoon vegetable oil,
    plus extra to serve
Pinch of salt

OPTIONAL FILLING
Chopped cooked prawns (shrimp),
    sliced spring onion (scallion)
    or chopped *char siu* (Cantonese
    barbecued pork)

Combine the rice flour, 400 ml (14 fl oz) water, sesame oil, vegetable oil and salt in a blender and blend until smooth. The batter should be lovely and milky white.

Use a jug or ladle to pour a thin layer of batter into a large rectangular microwave-safe container, then cover with a lid. Microwave the rice noodle sheet on high for around 4 minutes, then let it rest for 2 minutes. You may need to experiment with the microwave time. Meanwhile, lightly oil a serving plate and set aside.

At this point, you can add fillings such as cooked prawns, sliced spring onion or *char siu*. Use a spatula to carefully roll the rice noodle sheet up into a flat noodle shape. Transfer onto the oiled serving plate. Repeat with the remaining batter and filling. Clean the container between cooking each rice noodle sheet.

NOTES
You could also use a stick blender for the batter. The suggested microwave times above are for an 1100-watt microwave.

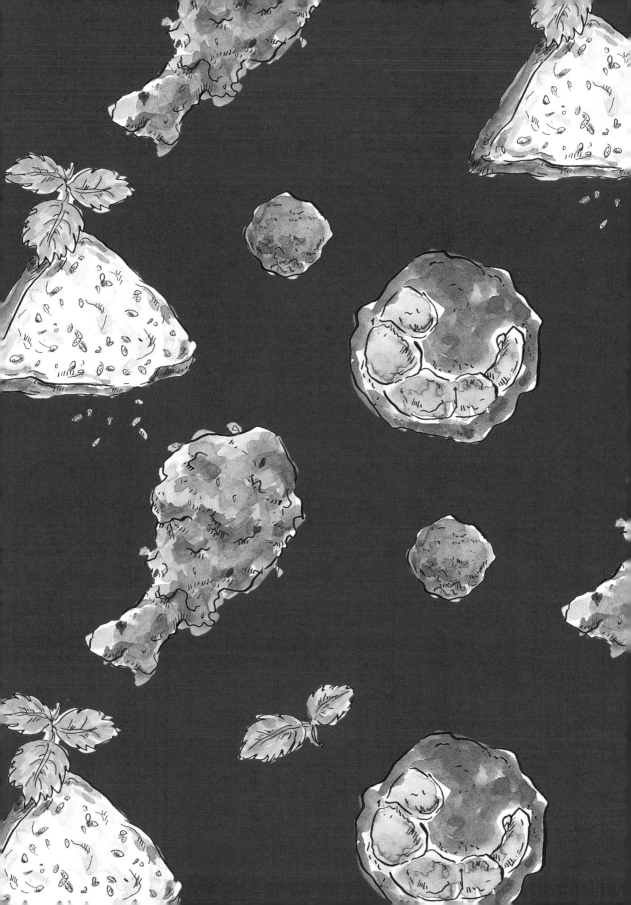

CHINESE-ISH SNACKS THAT FEEL KINDA WRONG

A VERY INAUTHENTIC PRAWN TOAST

This prawn toast recipe is special: it's an Asian-Australian version of the beloved yum cha classic. It's also an ode to hot summers spent eating plentiful fresh prawns with lemon wedges. There's a little nod to the strong Italian influence in Melbourne via the guanciale that you fold through the prawn mix for gloriously salty, porky morsels. You should always have a stash of seafood in your freezer, in case you want to whip up something delicious on a whim. Highly perishable seafood is often processed and snap-frozen on the boat, preserving it at its peak. It's incredibly cost-effective and convenient.

SERVES 4

2 tablespoons olive oil

2 cloves garlic, minced

120 g (4¼ oz) raw prawns (shrimp), peeled and deveined

20 g (¾ oz) guanciale or pancetta, finely chopped

40 g (1½ oz) pork mince (ground pork)

4 cm (1½ inch) piece ginger, grated

1 teaspoon cornflour (cornstarch)

2 teaspoons fish sauce

½ teaspoon ground white pepper

½ teaspoon salt

20 g (¾ oz) dill sprigs, finely chopped

Zest of ½ lemon

4 slices white bread

2 cups (500 ml) vegetable oil, for frying

Lemon cheeks, to serve

Warm the olive oil in a small frying pan and add the garlic. Fry over low heat until the garlic is soft, then set aside to cool.

Place the prawns, guanciale, pork mince, ginger, cornflour, fish sauce, white pepper and salt into a food processor and blitz to form a paste. Transfer to a bowl and add the softened garlic, along with the dill and lemon zest, and stir through.

Cut each slice of bread into four triangles. Spread the prawn mixture thickly over each triangle and set aside.

Heat the vegetable oil to 180°C (350°F) using a food thermometer to check the temperature, then deep-fry the prawn triangles in small batches until golden-brown. Drain using a slotted spoon and eat with a squeeze of lemon juice.

SICHUAN SAUSAGE SANGAS

I love a 'sausage sizzle', as we call them in Australia, where you can grab a barbecued,
slightly singed snag (sausage) wrapped in soft white bread, in exchange for a gold coin.
This recipe keeps the sizzle, the sausage and the white bread, but the similarities end
there. Instead, a flavourful, juicy, Sichuan peppercorn-spiced pork sausage is studded
with guanciale, smeared with Japanese mayonnaise and refreshed with lime juice.
Definitely not your average sausage sanga.

SERVES 4

450 g (1 lb) pork mince (ground pork)
50 g (1¾ oz) guanciale or pancetta,
  finely chopped
2 teaspoons grated ginger
2 tablespoons fish sauce
1 tablespoon light soy sauce
1 tablespoon Dijon mustard
2 teaspoons caster (superfine) sugar
1 tablespoon cornflour (cornstarch)
1 teaspoon iced water
Vegetable oil, for shallow frying

SPICE MIX

3 teaspoons Sichuan or
  Korean chilli flakes
2 teaspoons Sichuan peppercorns
1 teaspoon ground white pepper
½ teaspoon cumin seeds
½ teaspoon coriander seeds
½ teaspoon ground turmeric

TO ASSEMBLE

4 slices white bread
Coriander (cilantro) leaves
Mint leaves
Kewpie mayonnaise
Lime wedges

Place the pork mince in the freezer for 30 minutes before using.

To make the spice mix, place all of the ingredients in a small frying
pan and toast over low heat until very fragrant, taking care not to
burn the chilli flakes. If they turn too dark, start again. Set aside
to cool, then blitz into a fine powder using a food processor.

Add the chilled pork mince, guanciale, ginger, fish sauce, light soy
sauce, Dijon mustard, sugar, cornflour and iced water to the spice
mix and pulse until combined. The mixture should bounce back
when pressed. Refrigerate the sausage mixture for 2 hours.

Using wet hands, roll the sausage mixture into four 2 cm x 10 cm
(¾ inch x 4 inch) logs and refrigerate for at least 1 hour to set.

Heat a frying pan over medium heat and add enough vegetable oil
to evenly coat the base of the pan. Cook the sausages until they are
a deep golden-brown, rolling them around continuously for about
10 minutes.

To assemble, wrap the sausages in white bread with a generous
handful of fresh herbs, a decent smear of mayonnaise and a good
squeeze of lime juice.

CRISPY PRAWN BALLS WITH FERMENTED CHILLI DIP

All of the goodness of prawn toast in one perfect little bite! This recipe uses the same prawn mousse you might find on a slice of classic prawn toast, but rolled in panko and fried until crispy. Dunk it in a salty-spicy fermented chilli dip for the perfect snack.

SERVES 4

1⅔ cups (100 g) panko breadcrumbs
2 cups (500 ml) vegetable oil

PRAWN BALLS
400 g (14 oz) raw prawns (shrimp), peeled and deveined
1 egg white
1 teaspoon fish sauce
½ teaspoon salt
1 teaspoon caster (superfine) sugar
1 tablespoon cornflour (cornstarch)
1 teaspoon sesame oil
Ground white pepper, to taste

To make the prawn balls, place all of the ingredients into a food processor and blitz to form a smooth paste.

Place the breadcrumbs on a baking tray. Using wet hands, roll 1 tablespoon of the prawn paste into a ball, then roll the ball in the breadcrumbs. Repeat with the remaining paste.

Heat the vegetable oil in a frying pan to 170°C (325°F) using a food thermometer to check the temperature, then deep-fry the prawn balls in batches until golden. Drain and serve with fermented chilli dip (see below).

FERMENTED CHILLI DIP

1 tablespoon Hunan salted chilli (see page 93) or store-bought fermented chilli paste
1 teaspoon light soy sauce
1 teaspoon stock (see page 51) or use a good-quality store-bought stock
½ teaspoon sesame oil

Combine all the ingredients in a bowl. Stir and adjust the seasoning to taste.

STICKY GARLIC RIBS WITH FRESH CHILLI AND VINEGAR SAUCE

I'VE BEEN LET DOWN SO MANY TIMES BY THE STICKY-SWEET GLAZES OF FAUX ASIAN CUISINE. THEY'RE ALWAYS SO OVERPOWERINGLY SWEET THAT IT'S LIKE BEING FORCE-FED SPOONFULS OF SUGAR WHEN I'M INNOCENTLY TRYING TO EAT MY LUNCH. NOW WHEN I SEE THE WORD 'STICKY' ON A DISH, I RUN A MILE. IF YOU'RE FIRMLY IN THE 'I LOVE STICKY-SWEET GLAZES' CAMP, HOWEVER, DON'T LET ME STOP YOU FROM LIVING YOUR BEST LIFE.

WHILE STICKY TEXTURES ARE ALMOST ALWAYS ACHIEVED BY CARAMELISING SUGAR ON THE SURFACE OF YOUR FOOD, IT IS ACTUALLY POSSIBLE TO CREATE THE SAME EFFECT USING SAVOURY INGREDIENTS. THIS RECIPE USES CARAMELISED GARLIC AND CORNFLOUR (CORNSTARCH) FRIED TWICE TO CREATE THAT DELIGHTFUL GLUE-YOUR-FRONT-TEETH-TOGETHER EXPERIENCE. ASK YOUR BUTCHER TO CUT THE RIBS DOWN INTO SMALLER PIECES FOR YOU, BECAUSE MORE SURFACE AREA MEANS MORE MESSY, STICKY FUN. THE RIBS SHOULD MARINATE FOR A MINIMUM OF 6 HOURS, BUT IDEALLY OVERNIGHT, TO REALLY DEVELOP THEIR FLAVOUR BEFORE BEING FRIED. SERVE THEM WITH A DIPPING SAUCE FEATURING PLENTY OF FRESH CHILLI, CORIANDER (CILANTRO) AND RAW GARLIC, IN CASE YOU DIDN'T HAVE ENOUGH GARLIC TO BEGIN WITH.

I RECOMMEND INVESTING IN A FOOD THERMOMETER FOR SITUATIONS LIKE THIS, WHERE YOU NEED SOME DEGREE OF CONTROL OVER THE OIL TEMPERATURE. IF YOU DON'T HAVE ONE, IT HELPS TO DROP ONE PIECE OF FOOD IN AS YOUR TESTER. IF YOUR OIL IS HOT ENOUGH, IT SHOULD SIZZLE. IN THIS CASE, IT IS MUCH BETTER FOR YOUR OIL TO BE COOLER RATHER THAN HOTTER THAN THE DESIRED TEMPERATURE.

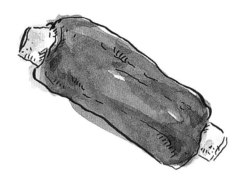

SERVES 4

1 head garlic, minced
1 cm (½ inch) piece ginger, minced
1 tablespoon dark soy sauce
1 tablespoon light soy sauce
1 tablespoon oyster sauce
500 g pork ribs (1 full rack), cut into
    3–4 cm (1¼–1½ inch) pieces
    (see Note)
½ cup (60 g) cornflour (cornstarch)
Vegetable oil, for deep-frying

DIPPING SAUCE

2 small red birdseye chillies,
    minced
1 teaspoon minced garlic
1 green chilli, minced
2 tablespoons light soy sauce
1 tablespoon sesame oil
½ teaspoon Chinkiang
    black vinegar
2 tablespoons chopped coriander
    (cilantro) leaves

Mix all of the ingredients
together and serve.

Rinse the minced garlic under running water, then drain and spread on a sheet of paper towel to dry. Removing the enzyme that coats the surface of chopped garlic helps to prevent it from burning, which is important for our purposes here.

Mix the garlic, ginger, soy sauces and oyster sauce in a large bowl. Add the pork ribs and thoroughly combine, then cover and allow to marinate in the fridge for anywhere between 6 and 24 hours.

Take the ribs out of the fridge at least 1 hour before cooking to bring them to room temperature. Add the cornflour to the bowl and mix well to combine.

Heat at least 5 cm (2 inches) of oil in a heavy-based saucepan to 150°C (300°F) using a food thermometer to check the temperature. Fry the ribs in small batches for 6–8 minutes, keeping the heat low. You're not trying to crisp or brown the ribs but confit them, so the temperature should remain below 150°C (300°F) to ensure the garlic doesn't burn and the ribs continue to cook at a gentle heat.

Once all of the ribs have been fried once, bring the oil up to 200°C (400°F), until smoking. Fry the ribs in batches for 20–30 seconds, moving them continuously to keep the garlic from burning. Be very careful at this stage, as the acrid flavour of burnt garlic is difficult to hide. Once the ribs are caramelised and golden, transfer them to a plate. Serve hot with the dipping sauce.

NOTE
Ask your butcher to cut your pork for you, if you like.

BEIJING HOT CHICKEN

I HAD A THEORY: IF YOU PUT CHICKEN THROUGH THE SAME THREE-DAY PROCESS AS NASHVILLE HOT CHICKEN (BRINING, BUTTERMILK BRINING, AND THEN DREDGING), BUT SWAPPED THE CAYENNE, PAPRIKA, ONION AND GARLIC FOR A DEEPLY AROMATIC NORTHERN CHINESE SPICE MIX, IT COULD BE PRETTY GOOD. WHILE WE'RE AT IT, WHY NOT USE THE KOREAN TECHNIQUE OF DREDGING AND FRYING, TOO? THAT COULD BE REALLY GOOD.

IT WASN'T JUST GOOD, IT WAS UTTERLY GLORIOUS. THE POTATO-STARCH DREDGE BECAME AN INCREDIBLY LIGHT AND CRISPY (NOT HARD AND CRUNCHY) COATING. THE DOUBLE-FRYING TECHNIQUE WAS SO EFFECTIVE THAT THE CHICKEN WAS STILL CRISPY THE NEXT DAY. THE INTENSITY OF THE SPICES IN THE BUTTERMILK BRINE PENETRATED RIGHT INTO THE CHICKEN, RESULTING IN PERFECTLY SEASONED, TENDER BITES. THEN, OF COURSE, THERE WAS THE SPICE MIX, THAT MAGNIFICENT SPICE MIX. THE WARM, ROASTY AROMAS OF CUMIN, GARLIC AND CHILLI TAKE YOU RIGHT TO THE SMOKY BACK ALLEYS OF BEIJING, WHERE THIS SAME SPICE MIX IS DUSTED OVER CRISP CHARCOAL-ROASTED MEATS.

I ALSO MANAGED TO CUT A WHOLE DAY OUT OF THE TRADITIONAL NASHVILLE PROCESS BY CONDENSING IT INTO TWO STEPS. ON DAY 1, YOU MAKE THE BUTTERMILK BRINE AND SUBMERGE THE CHICKEN IN IT. ON DAY 2, YOU DREDGE AND FRY. THE SPICINESS CAN BE ADJUSTED TO SUIT YOUR PERSONAL PREFERENCE, AS THE CHICKEN IS WELL SEASONED EVEN BEFORE YOU COAT IT IN THE CHILLI OIL AND SPICE MIX. WHEN I MAKE FRIED CHICKEN AT HOME, I ALWAYS DO HALF PLAIN, HALF SPICY, SO IT'S NOT ALL PAIN AND SUFFERING. I EAT MY FRIED CHICKEN BETWEEN TWO SLICES OF FLUFFY WHITE BREAD, WITH TINY PICKLED GREEN CHILLIES, MAYO AND A WEDGE OF LETTUCE TO COOL THE BURN. HOW YOU CHOOSE TO EAT YOURS IS ENTIRELY UP TO YOU.

SERVES 4

Vegetable oil, for deep-frying
2 tablespoons chilli oil (see page 94,
    or use Lao Gan Ma chilli oil)
1 teaspoon salt

BUTTERMILK BRINE

4 cups (1 litre) buttermilk
2 tablespoons salt
2 teaspoons chicken bouillon powder
1 teaspoon garlic powder
2 tablespoons Sichuan or regular
    chilli powder *(see Notes on page 38)*
8 skinless chicken thigh fillets

BEIJING SPICE MIX

2 teaspoons white peppercorns
1 teaspoon Sichuan peppercorns
3 teaspoons cumin seeds
1 teaspoon garlic powder
2 teaspoons Sichuan or regular
    chilli powder *(see Notes on page 38)*
2 teaspoons chilli flakes

POTATO-FLOUR DREDGE

1½ cups (265 g) potato flour
    (potato starch)
½ cup (75 g) plain (all-purpose) flour
1 teaspoon ground black pepper
1 teaspoon salt

DAY 1

To make the buttermilk brine, combine the buttermilk, salt, chicken
bouillon powder, garlic powder and chilli powder in a large bowl or
container. Ensure the container is deep enough so that the chicken
will be completely submerged. Place the chicken thighs into the
buttermilk brine, cover and refrigerate for 12–24 hours.

DAY 2

To make the Beijing spice mix, heat a small frying pan over low heat
and toast the white and Sichuan peppercorns and cumin seeds,
moving the pan continuously so that the spices toast evenly. When
the spices are lovely and aromatic, add the garlic powder, chilli
powder and chilli flakes and toast gently for 30 seconds. Allow the
spices to cool, then grind them into a coarse powder using a mortar
and pestle.

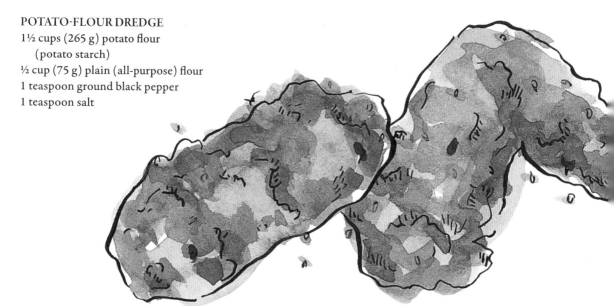

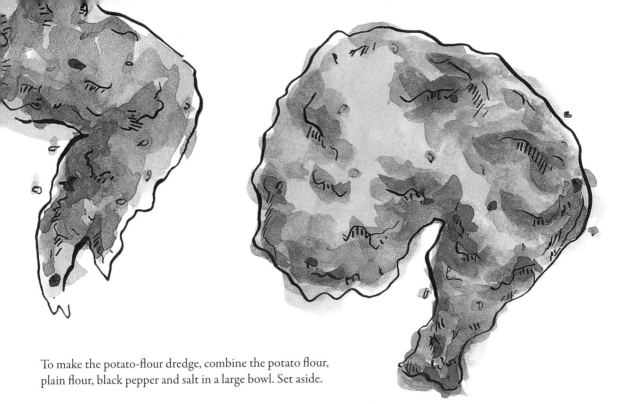

To make the potato-flour dredge, combine the potato flour, plain flour, black pepper and salt in a large bowl. Set aside.

Heat at least 6 cm (2½ inches) of vegetable oil in a large heavy-based saucepan to 160°C (215°F), using a food thermometer to check the temperature. Lift each piece of chicken out of the buttermilk brine and shake off the excess. Thoroughly coat the chicken in the potato-flour dredge, then carefully lower into the oil. Fry the chicken in batches, making sure the pieces don't touch each other or stick to the bottom of the pan. Fry for 5–6 minutes, until the crust is just set. Transfer to a wire rack to rest while the remaining chicken is fried.

When all of the pieces have been fried once, fry each batch a second time, until the coating is extra crispy, 6–7 minutes. Potato flour does not brown like plain flour does, so don't attempt to fry until golden. When you tap the coating and it is hard and crisp, the chicken is ready to drain on a wire rack. Reserve ½ cup (125 ml) of the hot frying oil.

Place 2 tablespoons of the Beijing spice mix in a heatproof bowl with the reserved frying oil, chilli oil and salt, and mix to combine. Add 2 chicken pieces to the bowl at a time and toss to coat in the spice and oil mix. Return the chicken to the wire rack and sprinkle generously with the remaining Beijing spice mix. Serve hot.

FIERY SICHUAN FONDUE

IT'S A WELL-ESTABLISHED FACT THAT PLENTY OF PEOPLE OF EAST ASIAN DESCENT SUFFER FROM LACTOSE SENSITIVITY. AND LET'S BE HONEST — FONDUE ISN'T REALLY CHINESE IN THE SLIGHTEST. SO YOU'RE PROBABLY WONDERING WHY THERE IS A FONDUE RECIPE IN THIS COOKBOOK. I'M A TOUCH LACTOSE-INTOLERANT MYSELF, BUT I RECKON THIS RECIPE IS WORTH THE PAIN.

IT MIGHT SEEM SIMPLE, BEING NOTHING MORE THAN CHEESE AND WINE MELTED TOGETHER, BUT FONDUE SPLITS EASILY. A WELL-MADE FONDUE SHOULD BE SILKY-SMOOTH AND REMAIN THAT WAY, EVEN WHEN HEATED. FOR SUREFIRE SUCCESS EVERY TIME, ADD CORNFLOUR (CORNSTARCH) TO THE MIX: IT STOPS THE PROTEINS IN THE CHEESE FROM COAGULATING, GUARANTEEING YOUR FONDUE STAYS SMOOTH AND SILKY.

IN THIS RECIPE, WE USE BEER INSTEAD OF THE TRADITIONAL HIGH-ACID WHITE WINE. BEER IS EXACTLY WHAT I'D BE DRINKING WITH THIS DISH, AS THE SAVOURINESS PAIRS BEAUTIFULLY WITH THE CHEESE. AS WITH ALL POPULAR SICHUAN DISHES, THIS FONDUE IS SERVED UNDER A BLAZE OF VIBRANT RED CHILLI OIL.

IF YOU DON'T HAVE A FANCY FONDUE SET-UP, USE A CAST-IRON SKILLET OR SOMETHING SIMILAR THAT RETAINS HEAT, AND POP IT BACK ON THE STOVE WHENEVER YOU NEED TO WARM IT UP. PILE THE FONDUE HIGH WITH FRESH HERBS AND CRACKED BLACK PEPPER, THEN DIP ANYTHING YOUR HEART DESIRES INTO IT. FONDUE IS TRADITIONALLY SERVED WITH CUBES OF STALE BREAD, PICKLED ONIONS AND CORNICHONS, BUT ANYTHING THAT WOULD BE IMPROVED BY BEING DUNKED IN FIERY CHEESE WILL DO. JUST MAKE SURE EVERYTHING IS BITE-SIZED.

SERVES 6

2 tablespoons cornflour (cornstarch)
300 g (10½ oz) Gruyère, grated
300 g (10½ oz) Comté, grated
2 cloves garlic, minced
300 ml (10½ fl oz) lager
1 tablespoon lemon juice
½ teaspoon salt
½ teaspoon ground white pepper
100 ml chilli oil (see page 94,
    or use Lao Gan Ma chilli oil)
Fresh dill, parsley and chives,
    roughly chopped
Cracked black pepper

TO SERVE
Pickled chillies
Bread, cut into cubes
Hot smoked sausages
Charcuterie
Boiled potatoes

Place the cornflour and cheeses in a bowl and toss to combine. Set aside.

Heat the garlic and lager in a pan over low heat and bring to a simmer. Add a handful of the cheese mixture at a time to the simmering beer and whisk vigorously, ensuring each addition is completely melted and emulsified before adding more.

Once all the cheese has been added and the mixture is thick and smooth, add the lemon juice, salt and white pepper and stir. If the mixture has turned into a blob of melted cheese with some separated liquid, don't worry. Simply increase the heat and whisk hard to bring it back together.

Transfer the cheese mixture to a fondue pot or cast-iron skillet. Dress liberally with the chilli oil, fresh herbs and cracked black pepper. If the fondue starts to set, simply pop it back on the stove and warm it up over low heat.

Serve the fondue with pickled chillies, bread, smoked sausages, charcuterie and boiled potatoes, for dipping.

PART THREE

My Love Language is a Fruit Platter

ON THE LOVE OF AN IMMIGRANT PARENT

JO : There are things about parenting that make it universally difficult, but I often struggle to imagine just how tough it must be for immigrant parents. To have all the uncertainties and anxieties about keeping a small human alive, while simultaneously being saddled with the burden of navigating an unfamiliar place, language and culture, and being far from your support network and family. It all seems insurmountable. And yet so many families embark on this journey every day, motivated by making a better life for the generation after them.

Immigrants face the added challenge of needing to learn enough about their new culture to fit in, while carrying the memories of where they came from. There is so much that I can only appreciate now that I am older than my parents were when they first arrived in this country: how lonely it must have been to be away from family and friends; how difficult it would have been to raise a small child while juggling so much work and study; and how they must have put all their own personal dreams on hold to get by.

Being raised in a western society, where spiritual and emotional wellbeing are held in the same esteem as economic security, contributed to the friction between my generation and my parents' generation. My idea of family life came from western sitcoms and movies, where baking cookies, being taken to the movies with friends, and camping holidays were all commonplace.

In contrast, my home life seemed to revolve exclusively around activities that strengthened the chances of my acceptance into a good school, and then my progression to a good university degree.

In addition, I vividly recall some of the more robust physical discipline that was enforced during this period. I carried this latent anger and resentment into adulthood, around the time that I also decided to reject the more traditional elements of my background.

It's easy to dwell on these perceived offences when you are too young and selfish; maturity almost has a way of arriving too late. All those things which, at the time, felt like acts of personal vilification were later revealed to be sacrificial acts of love. My parents' way of showing how much they cared for me manifested in spending all their time and money on extensive after-school tutoring, designed to further my academic success. It manifested in them skimping and saving in every other facet of their life so they could send me to a private school. My dad used to sit with me through every piano lesson and take notes so he would be better equipped to supervise my practice during the week. My mum would drive me to exam revision classes and wait for two hours in her car to save the petrol consumption of having to drive home and back again to pick me up.

The last time I was between apartments, I moved back home with my parents for eight weeks. While the close proximity resulted in the occasional clash, there was also the nightly ritual of a plate of sliced pear and peeled orange that would be delivered to my room – a silent, wordless replacement for any exculpatory conversation. One night, I noticed my mum was busy with work, and I decided to return the favour for the first time.

Immigrant parents often have to hold so much inside while they assimilate, shielding their pain and disappointments behind their love for their children. They often raise kids who can't even speak the same language as them, so words become obsolete to both parties, neither being able to confidently use them to express emotion. And perhaps it was hard to understand or to see at times, but it seems to me now that a worthy addition to the five love languages is a platter of carefully selected and prepared fruit, brought out at the end of a meal. It might just be the ultimate non-verbal demonstration of love.

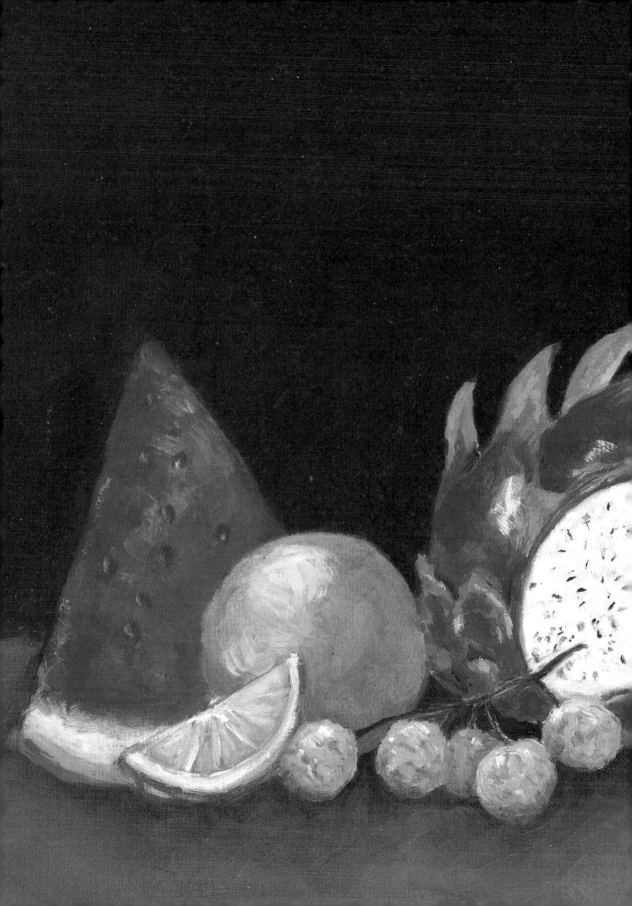

OLD CHINESE
FAVOURITES
AND
FOND FOOD
MEMORIES

Mum's Braised Ginger Chicken

If any dish were to taste like home to me, this would be it. Fragrant with toasted sesame oil, a little soy and plenty of warming ginger, this simple, comforting braise makes an appearance on our dinner table any time someone shows signs of illness. Served simply with steamed rice, it literally tastes like a warm hug from my mum.

SERVES 4

¼ cup (60 ml) sesame oil
6 cm (2½ inch) piece old ginger
   (see Note), skin on, sliced
6–8 chicken thigh fillets, cut in half
1 teaspoon salt
1 teaspoon caster (superfine) sugar
1 teaspoon light soy sauce
1 tablespoon Shaoxing wine
Steamed rice, to serve

Heat the sesame oil in a wok or a frying pan over medium heat, add the ginger and stir-fry until fragrant. Add the chicken pieces and stir-fry until they start to brown, 4–5 minutes.

Add the salt, sugar, 2½ tablespoons water and soy sauce and stir. Cover and allow to simmer for 7–8 minutes. Pour the Shaoxing wine over the top and simmer briefly, until the chicken is cooked through. Serve hot with steamed rice.

NOTE
Old ginger is spicier than regular young ginger and has a fibrous, dry texture. Find it at most Asian grocers. If you can't source any, use regular ginger instead.

CEREAL BUTTER PRAWNS

If you associate the word 'cereal' with Weet-Bix, Nutri-Grain or Froot Loops, then cereal butter prawns (麦片虾) might sound like a pretty horrid concept. In reality, this crunchy, buttery, aromatic savoury dish is another Singaporean *zi char* favourite. To achieve the crunchy coating, it's customary to use Nestum (a coarsely milled mixed-grain cereal) tossed through butter that has been spiked with birdseye chillies and aromatic curry leaves. It's nice to stick to the original method by keeping the shells on the prawns, as these impart a much deeper flavour. However, you're welcome to peel the prawns before cooking, if you like – just be wary of overcooking them.

SERVES 4

500 g (1 lb 2 oz) raw prawns (shrimp)
1 teaspoon salt
1 teaspoon caster (superfine) sugar
1 egg, whisked
2 tablespoons plain (all-purpose) flour
2 tablespoons cornflour (cornstarch)
Vegetable oil, for shallow frying, plus
    1 tablespoon extra
1 tablespoon milk powder
1 tablespoon chicken bouillon powder
1 cup (105 g) Nestum cereal *(see Note)*
    or quick oats
30 g (1 oz) butter
15 curry leaves
2 birdseye chillies, sliced

Use a pair of sharp kitchen scissors to trim the legs and feelers off the prawns. Place the prawns in a bowl and season with the salt and sugar. Pour the whisked egg over the top and toss to coat. Sift the flour and cornflour together over the prawns and stir to combine.

In a wok, heat enough oil to shallow-fry the prawns, until smoking. Fry the prawns in batches until crispy, then set aside to drain on a wire rack.

Mix the milk powder, chicken bouillon powder and Nestum or oats in a bowl to combine. Heat the extra oil and the butter in a frying pan over medium heat and add the curry leaves and sliced chilli, frying until fragrant. Add the Nestum or oats mixture and toast, continuously stirring, until golden. Add the prawns and toss to coat. Serve hot.

NOTE
You can find Nestum cereal at most Asian grocers. If you can't find it, use quick oats instead.

CEREAL
BUTTER
PRAWNS

SEE PAGE 175

NYONYA PORK AND CRAB MEATBALL SOUP

Also known as '*bakwan kepiting*', this is a traditional dish from the Peranakans of Singapore and Malaysia, whose cuisine is called *Nyonya*. Featuring tender crab and pork meatballs in a delicate broth that has been scented with roast garlic and spiked with coriander (cilantro), it can be enjoyed simply with a bowl of steamed rice. If you are picking your own crab meat, you'll need a fresh mud crab weighing around 1.2–1.5 kg (2 lb 11 oz–3 lb 5 oz). Alternatively, picked fresh crab meat can be purchased from good fishmongers.

SERVES 4

2 tablespoons vegetable oil

225 g (8 oz) canned bamboo shoots, drained

6 cloves garlic, minced

500 g (1 lb 2 oz) pork mince (ground pork)

400 g (14 oz) cooked crab meat

¼ teaspoon ground white pepper, plus extra to taste

2 tablespoons light soy sauce, plus extra

1 egg

8 cups (2 litres) stock (see page 51), or use a good-quality store-bought stock

Salt, to taste

½ bunch coriander (cilantro), leaves and roots separated

Steamed rice and sliced red chilli, to serve

Heat the oil in a large deep saucepan or stockpot over medium heat. Add the bamboo shoots and garlic and fry until fragrant. Turn the heat off.

Transfer half the fried bamboo shoots and garlic to a bowl. Allow to cool, then combine with the pork mince, crab meat, white pepper, soy sauce and egg. Let the mixture stand for 1 hour to marinate.

Add the stock to the pan containing the remaining bamboo shoots and garlic and bring to the boil over medium–high heat. Season with salt, extra soy sauce and white pepper. Add the coriander roots and reduce the heat to a simmer.

Shape the pork and crab mixture into large meatballs and carefully drop them into the simmering soup. When the meatballs float, they are ready.

Ladle the soup into four bowls and divide the meatballs between them. Garnish with coriander leaves and serve with steamed rice and sliced red chilli.

SICHUAN PEPPER CHICKEN WITH FRIED BASIL

The name of this dish is deceptive. You might expect a dish named after the Sichuan province to have originated there but Sichuan pepper chicken is actually a Teochew specialty. Teochew cuisine is influenced by the Cantonese tradition, with its delicate treatment of seafood and vegetables. The Teochew influence on food is also very strong in Singapore, which is where I first encountered this dish.

The recipe here uses a lively combination of fragrant Sichuan peppercorns and warm black peppercorns. It's usually served through a tumble of leafy greens called 'pearl vegetable', which are difficult to source. This version is served with crispy basil leaves instead.

SERVES 4

500 g (1 lb 2 oz) chicken thigh fillets, cut into bite-size pieces
2 teaspoons black peppercorns
2 teaspoons Sichuan peppercorns
1 tablespoon fish sauce
2 teaspoons dark soy sauce
1 tablespoon oyster sauce
1 tablespoon Shaoxing wine
Vegetable oil, for deep-frying
1 bunch basil, leaves picked, stems discarded
1 red chilli, thinly sliced
Steamed rice, to serve

MARINADE

1 teaspoon oyster sauce
½ teaspoon ginger juice
    (see Note on page 86)
2 teaspoons Shaoxing wine
1 egg white
30 g (1 oz) cornflour (cornstarch)

To make the marinade, combine all of the ingredients together in a bowl. Add the chicken and mix, then cover and leave in the fridge for 1–2 hours to marinate.

Toast the black and Sichuan peppercorns in a wok or frying pan over low heat until fragrant. Allow to cool, then crush with a mortar and pestle.

Combine the fish sauce, dark soy sauce, oyster sauce, Shaoxing wine and 2 tablespoons water in a bowl, and set aside.

Heat enough oil for deep-frying in a wok or heavy-based pan. Add the basil leaves and fry them briefly, just until they stop sizzling. Remove and set aside on paper towel to drain.

Stir the chicken through the marinade once more, then carefully deep-fry in batches for around 30 seconds. Remove and set aside.

Discard all but 2 tablespoons of oil from the wok and heat over high heat, until smoking. Add the crushed peppercorns and stir-fry briefly, then return the chicken to the wok with the fish sauce mixture and toss to coat in the sauce. Stir-fry over high heat until the sauce thickens and the chicken is cooked, 2–3 minutes. Add the sliced red chilli and stir through.

Transfer the chicken to a plate and sprinkle with the fried basil leaves. Serve with steamed rice.

GREAT DISHES FOR A CROWD

UYGHUR 'BIG PLATE' CHICKEN WITH HAND-PULLED NOODLES

AS A TEENAGER, I SPENT A FEW MONTHS IN CHINA WITH THE AUSTRALIAN FENCING TEAM, TRAINING AT THE SHANGHAI SPORTS SCHOOL. I WAS THE ONLY PERSON IN THE GROUP WHO SPOKE ANY MANDARIN, AND SO I SOMEHOW FOUND MYSELF WITH THE RESPONSIBILITY OF LEADING THE TEAM AROUND CHINA WITH MY AMATEUR-LEVEL SPOKEN MANDARIN. WE OFTEN ATE AT A SMALL NOODLE SHOP NEXT TO OUR ACCOMMODATION, WHICH I LATER REALISED WAS A NORTHERN CHINESE HAND-PULLED NOODLE SHOP. THE OWNERS WERE A SMALL UYGHUR FAMILY WHO WERE OVERWHELMED BY OUR DAILY VISITS. I DECIPHERED A FEW CHARACTERS HERE AND THERE TO ENABLE US TO ORDER SOME SIMPLE AND DELICIOUS NOODLE SOUPS, BUT IT WAS MOSTLY JUST LOOKING AT THE PICTURES ON THE WALLS AND POINTING.

ONE DAY, I WAS FEELING ADVENTUROUS AND ORDERED A VERY TASTY-LOOKING CHICKEN DISH FROM A PHOTO. HALF AN HOUR LATER, EVERYONE HAD RECEIVED AND PROCEEDED TO FINISH THEIR NOODLES, BUT MY DISH HAD YET TO ARRIVE. I HEARD A DISCONCERTING SQUAWKING SOUND FROM OUTSIDE THE RESTAURANT AND THEN, 15 MINUTES LATER, AN ENORMOUS PLATE OF CHICKEN, THICK HANDMADE NOODLES, POTATOES AND CHILLIES LANDED IN FRONT OF ME. THIS WAS MY FIRST ENCOUNTER WITH DA PAN JI (大盘鸡), LITERALLY, 'BIG PLATE CHICKEN'. I WAS PARTICULARLY TAKEN ABACK BY HOW FAMILIAR AND COMFORTING THE FLAVOURS WERE, AND HOW MUCH THEY REMINDED ME OF MY DAD'S KASHMIRI COOKING. THE UYGHURS ARE A PREDOMINANTLY MUSLIM, TURKIC ETHNIC GROUP. ORIGINATING FROM XINJIANG, CHINA, THEY LIVE ALONG WHAT WAS ONCE THE SILK ROAD, PLACING THEM IN GEOGRAPHIC PROXIMITY TO CENTRAL ASIA. SOMEHOW, IN A TINY RESTAURANT IN SHANGHAI, I FOUND FLAVOURS THAT TOOK ME HOME.

SERVES 6–8

HAND-PULLED NOODLES
(SEE NOTES)
1⅓ cups (200 g) plain
    (all-purpose) flour
Pinch of salt
Vegetable oil, for greasing

For the hand-pulled noodles, combine 100 ml (3½ fl oz) water with the flour and salt to make a rough dough. Knead for 10–12 minutes, until the dough becomes soft and smooth. Wrap the dough in plastic wrap and allow to rest for 1 hour.

Remove the dough from the plastic wrap and knead once more, until smooth – it is important to knead only in one direction to allow the gluten to relax and stretch easily. Wrap the dough again and allow to rest for 30 minutes.

Oil the bench and your hands, then roll the noodle dough out into a large rectangular sheet of 2–3 mm (1/16 – 1/8 inch) thickness. Use a knife to cut long 3 cm (1¼ inch) wide strips. Cover the noodles with plastic wrap until you're ready to cook them.

1 whole chicken, cut into
 small pieces *(see Notes)*
1 cup (250 ml) vegetable oil
2 teaspoons caster (superfine) sugar
4 cm (1½ inch) piece ginger, sliced
8–10 cloves garlic, minced
2 spring onions (scallions), sliced
3 star anise
1 teaspoon Sichuan peppercorns
1 teaspoon Kashmiri chilli powder
2 black cardamom pods
½ cinnamon stick
½ teaspoon sweet paprika
1 red chilli, sliced
2 green chillies, cut into diamonds
1 red capsicum (pepper), deseeded
 and cut into diamonds
2 large starchy potatoes, peeled and
 quartered
2 tablespoons light soy sauce
1 tablespoon chicken bouillon powder
2 teaspoons salt

Boil enough water to submerge the chicken in a large saucepan or stockpot and blanch the chicken pieces for 2–3 minutes. Drain and rinse with cold water, then leave to dry thoroughly on a paper towel.

Heat the oil in a wok or frying pan over medium heat and add the sugar. Stir-fry the sugar carefully until it turns into a dark caramel, then gently add the chicken pieces in batches. It is very important that the blanched chicken is dry before it is added to the pan, or the oil will splatter. Stir-fry the chicken pieces until they are coated in the caramel, then add the ginger, garlic and spring onion. Stir-fry until fragrant.

Add the spices, chillies, capsicum and potatoes and stir-fry for a further 3–4 minutes. Add 2 cups (500 ml) water, soy sauce, chicken bouillon powder and salt. Bring to the boil over medium–high heat, then cover and turn down the heat to low and braise for 20–25 minutes.

Bring a large saucepan of salted water to the boil. Use your fingertips to press each noodle strip to flatten it further, then grip each end and pull the strips gently to stretch them, taking care not to tear them. Drop the noodles into the water and cook for 1–2 minutes, or until they float. Drain and rinse with cold water, then arrange on a large plate.

Remove the lid from the braising chicken, taste and adjust the seasoning if necessary. The potatoes should be soft and the chicken should be lovely and tender. Ladle the braise over the noodles and serve immediately.

NOTES
If you don't want to make noodles, use 300 g (10½ oz) dried thick wheat noodles or knife-cut noodles (available at most Asian grocers), cooked according to the packet instructions. Ask your butcher to cut your chicken for you, if you like.

DONG PO BRAISED PORK

Braised pork is my death-row meal. Tender, rich and unctuous, and needing nothing more than steamed rice doused in the braising liquid to make a complete meal, this dish is the king – or emperor – of pork braises. The pork is braised exclusively in rice wine and aromats, with no water added. The result is the most tender, luxurious braise, which yields at the lightest touch. The distinctive red colour comes from caramelising the skin, and sometimes from the addition of red yeast rice, which I have omitted here.

SERVES 6–8

1–2 kg (2 lb 4 oz – 4 lb 8 oz) boneless
  pork belly, skin on
2 tablespoons vegetable oil
1 tablespoon caster (superfine) sugar
6 spring onions (scallions)
8 cm (3¼ inch) piece ginger, sliced
3 cups (750 ml) Shaoxing wine
½ cup (125 ml) light soy sauce
2 tablespoons dark soy sauce
10 g (⅓ oz) rock sugar (see Note)
Steamed rice, to serve

Place the pork belly in a large saucepan or stockpot of boiling water and blanch for 10 minutes. Skim any impurities from the surface, then drain the pork belly and place on a tray or plate in the fridge to chill for 10–15 minutes.

Heat the oil and sugar in a wok or frying pan over medium heat and stir-fry until the sugar turns into a dark caramel. Add the pork, skin-side down, and reduce the heat to medium–low. Caramelise the pork skin until it turns a dark golden colour, then transfer to a plate.

In a heavy-based saucepan (traditionally, we use a clay pot), lay the spring onions in a thick layer to cover the base and follow with the ginger slices. This will ensure the pork skin doesn't stick to the pan during the braising process. Lay the pork, skin-side down, over the spring onions and ginger. Pour the Shaoxing wine over the top, and add the soy sauces and rock sugar. Cover and bring to the boil, then reduce the heat and simmer for 90 minutes.

Turn the pork over so that it is skin-side up and braise for a further 90 minutes. Transfer to a serving plate. Reduce the braising liquid until it's thick enough to coat the back of a spoon, then pour it over the pork.

Let the pork cool slightly in the braising liquid and serve with rice.

NOTE
You can find rock sugar in the Asian aisle of well-stocked supermarkets or at most Asian grocers.

STIR-FRIED SAUCY CRAB VERMICELLI

THIS RECIPE IS INSPIRED BY A CRAB NOODLE DISH I ONCE HAD IN SINGAPORE AT A ZI CHAR RESTAURANT. WOK HEI (OR 'WOK BREATH'), THE COMPLEX, CHARRY FRAGRANCE CREATED BY STIR-FRYING OVER EXTREMELY HIGH HEAT, FEATURES HEAVILY IN THIS COOKING STYLE. THE CRAB VERMICELLI I ORDERED CONTAINED HUGE, MEATY CHUNKS OF MUD CRAB PEEKING THROUGH A MOUNTAIN OF RICE VERMICELLI NOODLES, SLICKED WITH A RICH SEAFOOD GRAVY. IT WAS UNBELIEVABLY DELICIOUS.

IT'S A LITTLE HARDER FOR THE HOME COOK TO PROCURE LIVE MUD CRAB, AND I DON'T ENCOURAGE DISPATCHING CRUSTACEANS AT HOME. THIS IS BECAUSE MOST HOME COOKS LACK THE KNOW-HOW TO DO IT HUMANELY AND MAY END UP CAUSING MORE SUFFERING TO THE CRAB THAN IS NECESSARY. IF YOU DO WISH TO DISPATCH THE CRAB YOURSELF, POP IT IN THE FREEZER FOR AT LEAST 1 HOUR TO LOWER ITS BODY TEMPERATURE AND PUT IT TO SLEEP. THEN PLACE IT ON A CHOPPING BOARD AND USE THE TIP OF A HEAVY, SHARP KNIFE TO PIERCE QUICKLY THROUGH ITS BRAIN, BETWEEN THE EYES. THIS WILL KILL THE CRAB INSTANTLY.

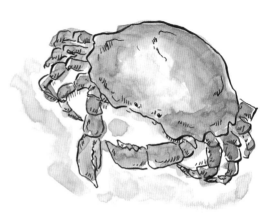

A MUCH LESS DAUNTING OPTION IS TO BUY FROZEN RAW CRAB, WHICH IS FAIRLY EASY TO TRACK DOWN. I USUALLY HAVE A BOX OF BLUE SWIMMER CRABS IN THE FREEZER, AS THEY ARE AFFORDABLE AND PACKED FULL OF FLAVOUR. I ALSO SAVE THE HEADS AND SHELLS WHENEVER I'M COOKING PRAWNS (SHRIMP) AND KEEP THEM IN THE FREEZER FOR STOCKS AND SAUCES. IF YOU DON'T HAVE ANY ON HAND, YOU CAN LEAVE THEM OUT OF THIS RECIPE, OR USE THE SHELLS AND HEADS FROM A HANDFUL OF PRAWNS WHILE KEEPING THE MEAT FOR ANOTHER USE.

SO WE START THIS RECIPE BY MAKING A RICH, AROMATIC PRAWN STOCK. IF, FOR SOME DELIGHTFUL REASON, YOU ALREADY HAVE PRAWN OR SHELLFISH STOCK ON HAND, YOU ARE MOST WELCOME TO USE IT AS THE BASE INSTEAD OF CHICKEN STOCK. THE MORE FLAVOUR YOU CAN PACK INTO THE SAUCE, THE BETTER.

STIR-FRIED SAUCY CRAB VERMICELLI CONT.

SERVES 6

3 cups (750 ml) vegetable oil for
    deep-frying, plus 1 tablespoon
    extra
2 x 5 cm (2 inch) pieces ginger, sliced
200 g (7 oz) prawn (shrimp) heads
    and shells
½ cup (125 ml) Shaoxing wine
    or brandy
8 cups (2 litres) stock (see page 51),
    or use a good-quality
    store-bought stock
2 raw mud crabs or 3 blue swimmer
    crabs, cleaned, claws and legs
    separated from body
½ cup (60 g) cornflour (cornstarch)
4 spring onions (scallions), cut into
    4 cm (1½ inch) lengths
8 cloves garlic, thinly sliced
2 tablespoons oyster sauce
2 tablespoons dark soy sauce
1 tablespoon light soy sauce
1 teaspoon chicken bouillon powder
1 teaspoon ground white pepper
200 g (7 oz) dried rice vermicelli,
    soaked in cold water for 30 minutes
    and then drained
Sliced red chilli, to serve

Heat the 1 tablespoon vegetable oil in a wok over medium heat, add the ginger and fry until fragrant. Add the prawn heads and shells and stir-fry, crushing them in the pan as you go. When they turn a dark golden colour, add the Shaoxing wine or brandy and deglaze. Add the stock and bring to the boil. Simmer, uncovered, over low heat for 30 minutes, then strain the stock, discarding the solids.

Heat the deep-frying oil in the cleaned wok over medium–high heat. Dust the crab pieces thoroughly in cornflour and deep-fry for 2–3 minutes, until the shells turn orange. Remove and set aside.

Remove all but 2 tablespoons of oil from the wok. Add the spring onion and garlic and fry until aromatic. Add the oyster sauce and soy sauces and stir for 10 seconds, then return the prawn stock to the wok. Add the chicken bouillon powder and white pepper.

Bring to the boil, add the crab and simmer for 2 minutes. Add the vermicelli, cover and simmer for 5 minutes, until the crab is cooked through and the noodles are soft. Stir thoroughly, then transfer to a large platter and serve with the sliced red chilli.

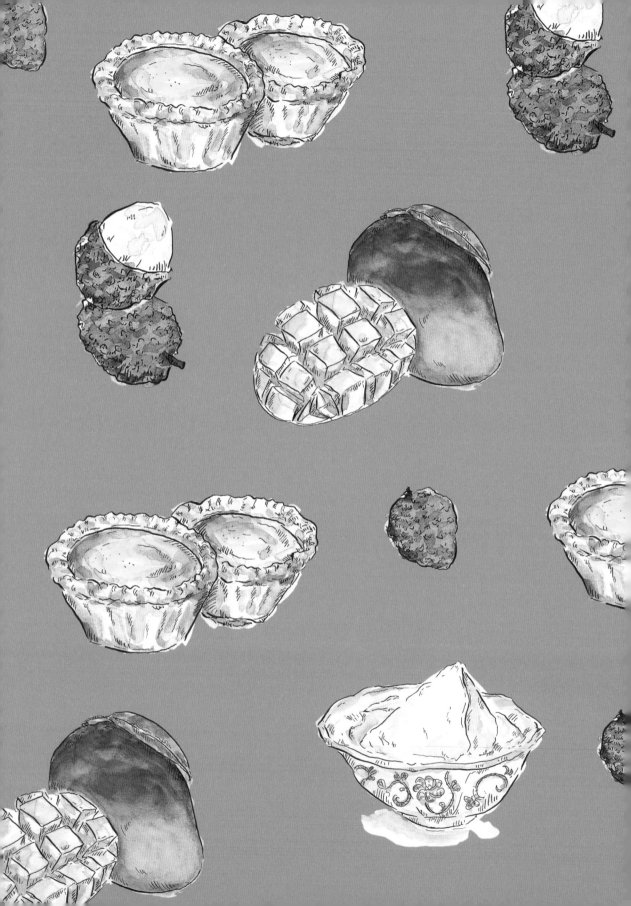

A FEW DESSERTS WE DON'T HATE

MANGO PUDDING

No matter how full I am at yum cha, I always have space for a mango pudding.
My sister and I – stuffed full of prawn *har gao* and fried beancurd skin rolls – only need
to nod and say, *'share?'* when the dessert trolley rolls around, before together happily
tucking into a soft, perfect little pudding doused in evaporated milk.
It tastes like happiness and nostalgia to me.

**MAKES 1 LARGE PUDDING
OR 6–8 SMALL ONES**

2 x 85 g (3 oz) packets mango-
    flavoured jelly crystals *(see Note)*
230 ml (7¾ fl oz) boiling water
100 ml (3½ fl oz) cold water
1 cup (250 ml) evaporated milk,
    plus extra to serve
2 mangoes, 1 peeled and blended,
    1 peeled and diced, to serve

Combine the jelly crystals and boiling water in a large bowl and
whisk to dissolve. Add the cold water, evaporated milk and blended
mango and stir to combine.

Pour into 1 large jelly mould, or 6–8 smaller moulds, and chill in
the fridge for 3–4 hours or until set.

Once the pudding is set, carefully immerse the mould in hot water
to loosen, and turn the pudding out onto a plate. Drizzle with
the extra evaporated milk and serve with diced mango.

NOTE
I use Aeroplane jelly. Yes, the one with the song.

soft tofu pudding with ginger scented syrup

I absolutely adore tofu pudding (豆腐花) – it is so comforting and beautifully delicate. It's eaten as a savoury breakfast in some parts of China, but is more widely enjoyed as a sweet dessert. Traditionally, the pillowy-soft curds are made by coagulating freshly pressed soy milk with gypsum powder, but the process can be simplified by using agar instead.

I can't emphasise enough how important it is to use fresh soy milk in this recipe – it is bright and refreshing and quite unlike the cardboard-flavoured nonsense you find at the supermarket.

SERVES 4

2 cups (500 ml) unsweetened fresh soy milk *(see Notes)*
5 g (⅛ oz) agar strips *(see Notes)*, soaked in cold water for 15 minutes and then squeezed dry

GINGER SYRUP
150 g (5½ oz) rock sugar *(see Note on page 189)*
2 cm (¾ inch) piece ginger, skin on

Place the soy milk in a large saucepan over medium heat and bring to the boil, taking care not to let it boil over. Squeeze the excess water from the agar, then add it to the soy milk and whisk to dissolve. Stir until you can no longer see pieces of agar floating, about 2 minutes. Remove from the heat and strain into a large container. Refrigerate for about 1 hour, or until set.

To make the ginger syrup, crush the rock sugar and ginger with a mortar and pestle and place into a small saucepan with 100 ml (3½ fl oz) water. Simmer over medium heat until the sugar has dissolved and the syrup has reduced slightly. Allow to cool with the ginger still in it, then strain and keep warm.

Use a ladle to scoop a large portion of tofu pudding into each bowl. Spoon the ginger syrup generously over the top and serve.

NOTES
You can find fresh soy milk and agar strips at most Asian grocers and some specialty grocers.

cheat's egg custard tarts

YOU'LL KNOW BY NOW THAT MOST OF MY COOKING REVOLVES
AROUND MY INHERENT IMPATIENCE (READ: LAZINESS). WHEN
I AM HIT WITH A CRAVING FOR SOMETHING SPECIFIC, I WANT IT
AS SOON AS POSSIBLE. THAT BEING SAID, MY LITTLE HACKS AND
SHORTCUTS COME FROM A GOOD PLACE, AND I WOULDN'T MAKE
ANY ADJUSTMENTS THAT RESULTED IN A SUB-PAR RECIPE. I HAVE
SOME PRIDE, AFTER ALL.

THE HUMBLE CUSTARD TART MAKES APPEARANCES IN MANY
DIFFERENT CULTURES, MOST FAMOUSLY AS THE PORTUGUESE
PASTEL DE NATA. THE EGG CUSTARD TART MADE ITS WAY TO HONG
KONG FROM THE NEARBY PORTUGUESE COLONY OF MACAO AND THE
CANTONESE TRANSFORMED IT BY ADDING MORE EGG YOLKS AND
DECREASING THE SUGAR AND DAIRY. THE RESULT IS A DELICATE,
EGGY CUSTARD WITH ONLY A GENTLE SWEETNESS, ENCASED IN
A FLAKY TART SHELL. TRADITIONAL CHINESE PUFF PASTRY IS
INCREDIBLY DIFFICULT TO MAKE. USING READY-MADE SHORTCRUST
PASTRY IS FOOLPROOF AND PUTS A STILL-WARM, FRESHLY BAKED
EGG CUSTARD TART IN EASY REACH OF EVERYONE.

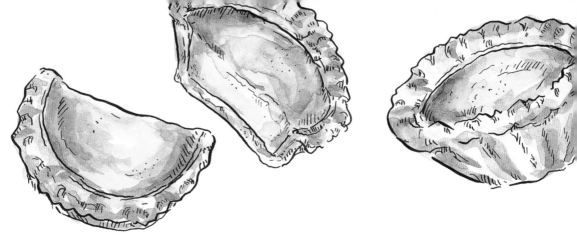

MAKES 12

Vegetable oil, for brushing
2 sheets shortcrust pastry

CUSTARD
⅓ cup (75 g) caster (superfine) sugar
150 ml (5 fl oz) hot water
2 eggs
¼ cup (60 ml) sweetened
    condensed milk
½ teaspoon vanilla extract

For the custard, dissolve the sugar in the hot water in a saucepan over low heat, stirring to make a syrup. In a bowl, whisk the eggs, condensed milk and vanilla together to combine. While whisking continuously, slowly pour the sugar syrup into the egg mixture. Strain into a jug and allow to stand until the air bubbles dissipate. Set aside.

Preheat the oven to 200°C (400°F).

Lightly brush a 12-hole muffin tin or 12 fluted individual tart tins with oil. Cut the pastry sheets into 12 even squares and press into the greased tins, trimming off any excess. Chill in the fridge for 15–20 minutes.

Line the pastry shells with baking paper and fill with pastry weights or uncooked rice. Blind-bake for 10 minutes, then carefully remove the paper and weights and bake for another 3–4 minutes, until golden. Set aside to cool.

Reduce the oven temperature to 140°C (275°F) and divide the custard equally between the shells.

Bake the tarts on the lowest shelf of your oven for 20–25 minutes, until the filling is just set. Remove from the oven and allow to rest for about 15 minutes. Enjoy the custard tarts while they're warm.

CHEAT'S
EGG CUSTARD
TARTS

SEE PAGE 200

PUMPKIN
CAKES
SEE PAGE 204

PUMPKIN CAKES

JO: I AM PERHAPS THE MORE VOCAL HATER OF ASIAN DESSERTS. THE FLAVOURS ARE OFTEN TOO SWEET, NOT SWEET ENOUGH, OR JUST PLAIN UNAPPETISING (LIKE, WHY IS RED BEAN SO PREVALENT?). AS DAVID CHANG SAYS IN HIS PODCAST CALLED LEFTOVERS, SCHOOL LUNCHES, DINING SOLO, AND MSG POPCORN: 'DON'T GET ME STARTED ABOUT RED BEAN. OF ALL THE F*CKING THINGS WE HAD TO GET WRONG IN ASIAN CUISINE, IT'S RED BEAN. WE COULDN'T HAVE FIGURED OUT CHOCOLATE OR BUTTER ...'

THEN THERE'S THE TEXTURAL ASPECT: AT THE END OF THE MEAL AT YUM CHA, THERE JUST SEEMS TO BE AN ENDLESS STREAM OF WOBBLY PUDDINGS, CUSTARDS AND JELLIES. LUCKILY, THE DEEP-FRYER ARRIVES TO SAVE THE DAY.

PUMPKIN CAKES ARE THAT PERFECT MIX OF CRUNCHY OUTER SHELL AND SWEET, SLIGHTLY DOUGHY CENTRE. THE GLUTINOUS RICE FLOUR ADDS A YIELDING BITE AND ELASTICITY, AND THE SESAME-SEED COATING MAKES THINGS EVEN MORE MOREISH, OR AS WE SAY IN CHINESE, 香.

**MAKES 15–20
SMALL CAKES**

300 g (10½ oz) pumpkin flesh
    (about 1 small pumpkin), peeled,
    deseeded and cut into thin,
    even slices
2 tablespoons icing
    (confectioners') sugar
1¼ cups (200 g) glutinous rice flour
Vegetable oil, for deep-frying
½ cup (75 g) sesame seeds

Place the pumpkin in a microwave-safe container and cook on high for 8 minutes, until very soft. Alternatively, you could steam the pumpkin for 25–30 minutes, until very soft. Drain any excess water from the flesh, place in a blender and blend into a puree. Add the icing sugar, adjust for your desired level of sweetness and blend once more.

Transfer the pumpkin puree to a bowl and add the glutinous rice flour in increments, working the mixture into a dry dough with your hands. You may need to add more flour depending on the water content of your pumpkin. The dough shouldn't stick to your hands.

In a wok or heavy-based pan, heat the oil to 160°C (315°F), using a food thermometer to check the temperature.

To make the cakes, roll the pumpkin dough into balls about the size of a ping pong, then flatten each into a 1.5 cm (⅝ inch) disc. Lightly dampen the surface of each cake with a little water and coat with sesame seeds. Working in batches, gently slide the cakes into the hot oil and fry until golden-brown, about 5–6 minutes.

After all the cakes have been fried once, fry them a second time for about 20 seconds to form a lasting crispy shell. Set aside to cool briefly before serving.

Lychee Plum Wine Shaved Ice

Japanese *kakigori*, Malaysian *ice kacang*, Korean *bingsoo*, Filipino *halo-halo* – nearly every Asian country has their own version of a shaved ice dessert. They almost always feature a majestic froth of fluffy ultra-fine ice shavings topped with flavoured syrups, jellies, sweet beans, condensed milk and other textural delights.

**MAKES 2, TO SHARE
BETWEEN 4**

PLUM WINE ICE
2 cups (500 ml) white grape juice
Pinch of salt
100 ml (3½ fl oz) Japanese plum wine

SUGAR SYRUP
½ cup (110 g) caster (superfine) sugar
Zest of 1 orange

LYCHEE JELLY
5 g (⅛ oz) agar strips (*see Notes on
    page 199*), soaked for 15 minutes in
    cold water and then squeezed dry
⅓ cup (75 g) caster (superfine) sugar
Juice from 1 can lychees,
    fruit reserved for assembly

CHANTILLY TOPPING
100 ml (3½ fl oz) single (pure) cream
1 tablespoon icing
    (confectioners') sugar

TO ASSEMBLE
Reserved fruit from 1 can lychees

To make the plum wine ice, place the grape juice and salt in a small saucepan over very low heat to dissolve the salt. Add the plum wine and stir, then pour into a large freezerproof container and freeze for 6–8 hours. Once frozen, use a fork to scratch the top layer of ice in one direction and then across in the other direction to make fine crystals. Scrape off the layer of ice crystals into another container and repeat the scratching and scraping process. Return the shaved ice to the freezer until you are ready to assemble.

To make the sugar syrup, place the sugar, 1 cup (250 ml) water and orange zest in a saucepan over medium–high heat and bring to the boil. Stir to dissolve the sugar and reduce by half. Remove the syrup from the heat and allow to cool.

To make the lychee jelly, place the pre-soaked agar strips, sugar and 400 ml (14 fl oz) water in a saucepan over medium heat and stir until the sugar has dissolved. Add the lychee juice, stir and remove from the heat. Pour the mixture into a 2 cm (¾ inch) deep tin and refrigerate until firm, about 1 hour. Turn the jelly out onto a board and cut into 1 cm (½ inch) cubes. Set aside.

To make the chantilly topping, whisk the cream and sugar together to form soft peaks.

To assemble, divide the lychees between two chilled shallow bowls. Top with a layer of shaved ice and some jelly cubes. Repeat with more shaved ice and jelly cubes, building as much height as possible.

Serve the shaved ice topped with sugar syrup and a generous dollop of the chantilly topping.

wonton-skin cannoli with sweet potato custard

Store-bought wonton wrappers are a blessing in disguise. They're a great way to make fake tortellini, and they make excellent crackers when deep-fried. I once ate a wonton wrapper that had been fried and dusted in icing sugar, crostoli-style, and realised it had plenty more untapped potential as a dessert. I can't be the first person to discover that you can turn wonton wrappers into cannoli shells, and I definitely won't be the last.

SERVES 10

10 white wonton wrappers *(see Note)*
    or 10 cannoli shells
Vegetable oil, for deep-frying
Caster (superfine) sugar,
    for coating

First, make the cannoli shells. If you're using wonton wrappers, use your fingertip to moisten one edge of each wrapper with a little water and fold one side over the other to create a tube. Pinch the edges together to seal. Repeat with the remaining wrappers, then set aside.

In a heavy-based saucepan, heat enough oil to deep-fry the cannoli to 170°C (325°F), using a food thermometer to check the temperature. If using wonton wrappers, insert the handle of a wooden spoon through one of the wonton tubes and carefully lower it into the hot oil. Gently rotate the spoon until the entire shell has puffed, then remove it and repeat with the remaining wrappers. Drain the shells on a rack and then roll in the sugar while hot. Set aside to cool.

If you're using cannoli shells, fry 2–3 at a time, continuously turning the shells to ensure they crisp up evenly. If your oil is at the correct temperature, it should take 3–4 minutes to fry each cannoli until it's puffed and golden.

The shells can be stored, unfilled, in an airtight container for 3–4 days.

NOTE
Make sure you buy white wonton wrappers, not the yellow variety.

SWEET POTATO CUSTARD
455 ml (16 fl oz) full-cream
    (full-fat) milk
⅔ cup (150 g) caster (superfine) sugar
⅓ cup (40 g) cornflour (cornstarch)
3 eggs, plus 1 extra yolk
300 g (10½ oz) boiled and mashed
    sweet potato (kumara)
Icing (confectioners') sugar,
    for dusting

For the sweet potato custard, combine 400 ml (14 fl oz) of the milk and half the sugar in a small saucepan over medium heat and bring to a simmer to dissolve the sugar. Milk has a tendency to boil over, so watch it carefully.

Whisk the cornflour, remaining milk and sugar, eggs and extra yolk together in a bowl until combined. Slowly pour in the hot milk, whisking continuously so the eggs don't scramble. Pour the entire mixture back into the saucepan and cook over low heat until it thickens, stirring continuously with a spatula.

Strain through a fine sieve into a clean bowl. Cover with plastic wrap and refrigerate until set, about 30 minutes.

When the custard has set, place it in a mixing bowl with the mashed sweet potato and beat until smooth, using a stand mixer if you have one. If not, a stick blender or whisk are fine to use. Fill a piping bag fitted with a wide nozzle with the sweet potato custard and chill until you're ready to use it.

For maximum crispness, serve the cannoli within an hour of filling them. Pipe the custard into the shells from both ends, dust with icing sugar and eat immediately.

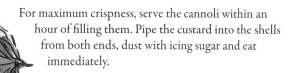

NYONYA-STYLE SAGO PUDDING

This simple, pretty and delicious version of sago pudding hails from Southeast Asia. Fragrant with pandan and coconut milk, the dark palm sugar imparts lovely caramelised flavours to the delicate sago pearls. This is a classic dessert from the Peranakans of Singapore and Malaysia.

SERVES 2

⅔ cup (120 g) dark palm sugar (*gula melaka*), chopped
1½ tablespoons caster (superfine) sugar
1 pandan leaf, knotted (optional)
80 g (2¾ oz) sago, cooked according to the packet instructions
100 ml (3½ fl oz) coconut milk

Place the palm sugar, caster sugar, pandan leaf (if using) and 100 ml (3½ fl oz) water in a small saucepan over low heat. Cook, stirring continuously, for 5–6 minutes or until the sugar dissolves, then bring to a simmer and cook for another 2 minutes. Remove from the heat and allow to infuse for 10 minutes, then strain the syrup, discarding the pandan leaf.

Divide the sago between bowls and spoon the coconut milk over the top. Drizzle the palm sugar syrup over the puddings and serve.

HONG KONG-STYLE SAGO PUDDING

The bright, fruity and rich flavours of this sago pudding are reminiscent of mango pudding. The pops of citrus from the pomelo, and the chunks of sweet mango, make this one of my favourite desserts of all time, particularly during mango season. If you have difficulty finding pomelo, ruby grapefruit is a good substitute.

SERVES 2

250 g (9 oz) diced mango,
  plus extra to serve
⅓ cup (80 ml) evaporated milk
1 teaspoon caster (superfine) sugar,
  to taste (optional)
60 g (2¼ oz) sago, cooked according
  to the packet instructions
2½ tablespoons coconut milk
2 tablespoons pomelo pulp *(see Note)*,
  or 1 tablespoon ruby
  grapefruit pulp

Place the mango, evaporated milk and ⅓ cup (80 ml) water in a food processor and blitz into a puree. At this point, taste for sweetness. If the mango is lovely and sweet, don't add any additional sugar. Otherwise, add the caster sugar and blitz once more in the food processor, until the sugar has completely dissolved.

To assemble, stir the sago and mango puree together to combine. Divide between two chilled serving bowls and drizzle with the coconut milk. Garnish with the extra diced mango and plenty of pomelo pulp.

NOTE
To prepare the pomelo, break it into segments, peel off the membrane (pith) and discard, then separate the pulp.

ACKNOWLEDGEMENTS

ROSHEEN: To Jo, of course, for agreeing – good-naturedly – to embark on this journey with me, and for being the more patient, diplomatic and contactable half of our duo. Only you could bring the beautiful nuances of our Asian-Australian identities to life.

To the thousands of people who supported us during the pandemic, who loved and accepted our *Isol(Asian) Cookbook* with open minds and hearts. To the inimitable Shannon Martinez, for her blind trust and for allowing me to create a menu based on our *Isol(Asian)* series for her formidable restaurant.

To Jane Morrow, for giving us the platform to tell our story. To Armelle Habib and Lee Blaylock, for seeing the vision as clearly as we did. To Mariam Digges – you have the patience of a saint and were a dream to work with. To Hannah Green, for seeing into the future and giving me everything I needed to achieve it.

To my parents, Raj and Tina; my sister, Roshali; and my brother-in-law, Michael – for your unwavering support and endless wisdom.

JO: I'd like to acknowledge my oversized desk – a lucky find last year during hard rubbish week; my ceramic paint palette, gifted by my best friend, Sisi; and the Kendall Hi White Ivory Board Smooth paper (gladly recycled from Paperlust), which I did all the illustrations on. Also providing crucial background support were: *Midsomer Murders*, Lotus Biscoff spread on crumpets, and *Hadestown (Original Broadway Cast Recording)*.

And Rosheen, the one who I started this journey with. From the very first messages between us in March 2020 – with ideas of collaboration on some fun projects to keep ourselves busy – to the surreal experience of having book offer meetings with Jane and the team at Murdoch Books months later. I would probably still be watching *Tiger King* if it weren't for your ideas and endless encouragement.

INDEX

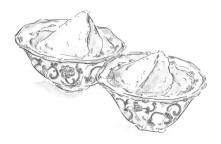

Published in 2022 by Murdoch Books, an imprint of Allen & Unwin

Murdoch Books Australia
83 Alexander Street
Crows Nest NSW 2065
Phone: +61 (0)2 8425 0100
murdochbooks.com.au
info@murdochbooks.com.au

Murdoch Books UK
Ormond House
26–27 Boswell Street
London WC1N 3JZ
Phone: +44 (0) 20 8785 5995
murdochbooks.co.uk
info@murdochbooks.co.uk

For corporate orders and custom publishing,
contact our business development team at
salesenquiries@murdochbooks.com.au

Publisher: Jane Morrow
Editorial Manager: Virginia Birch
Design Manager: Megan Pigott
Designer: Sarah Odgers
Editor: Mariam Digges
Illustrator: Joanna Hu
Photographer: Armelle Habib
Stylist: Lee Blaylock
Home Economists: Meryl Batlle/Josh Nicholson
Production Director: Lou Playfair

Colour reproduction by Splitting Image Colour
Studio Pty Ltd, Clayton, Victoria
Printed by C&C Offset Printing Co. Ltd., China

Text © Rosheen Kaul and Joanna Hu 2022
The moral right of the author has been asserted.
Design © Murdoch Books 2022
Photography © Armelle Habib 2022
Illustrations © Joanna Hu 2022

IMPORTANT: Those who might be at risk from the
effects of salmonella poisoning (the elderly, pregnant
women, young children and those suffering from
immune deficiency diseases) should consult their
doctor with any concerns about eating raw eggs. Please
ensure that all seafood and beef to be eaten raw or
lightly cooked are very fresh and of the highest quality.

*We acknowledge that we meet and work on the
traditional lands of the Cammeraygal people of the
Eora Nation and pay our respects to their elders
past, present and future.*

OVEN GUIDE: You may find cooking times vary
depending on the oven you are using. For fan-forced
ovens, as a general rule, set the oven temperature to
20°C (70°F) lower than indicated in the recipe.

TABLESPOON MEASURES: We have used 20 ml
(4 teaspoon) tablespoon measures. If you are using a
15 ml (3 teaspoon) tablespoon add an extra teaspoon
of the ingredient for each tablespoon specified.

ISBN 978 1 92235 179 1 Australia
ISBN 978 1 91166 847 3 UK

Every reasonable effort has been made to trace the
owners of copyright materials in this book, but in
some instances this has proven impossible. The
author(s) and publisher will be glad to receive
information leading to more complete
acknowledgements in subsequent printings of the
book and in the meantime extend their apologies
for any omissions.

A catalogue record for this book is
available from the National Library
of Australia

10 9 8 7 6 5 4 3 2 1

A catalogue record for this book is available from
the British Library

MIX
Paper from
responsible sources
FSC® C008047

Mum's Braised Ginger Chicken

cheat's egg custard

CR

BURNT SPRING ONION OIL NOODLES

NYONYA PORK AND CRAB MEATBALL SOUP

BRAISED SEAFO

VERMICELLI

stir-fried garlic shoots with jamón

SICHUAN-STYLE COLD NOODLES

ANTS CLIMBING NOODLES

UYGHUR 'BIG PLATE' CHICKEN WITH HAND-PULLED NOODLES

wonton-skin cannoli w

sweet potato custard

THREE EARTHLY TREASURES

CHAR KWAY TEOW CEREAL BUTTER PRAWN

chilli oil

STIR-FRIED TOMATO & EGG

STIR-FRIED SAU

CRAB VERMICELLI

FRIED C

SPICED

EGG FRIED RICE Lychee Plum Wine

Shaved Ice FISH

PORK AND PRAWN WONTONS

SICHUAN TIGER-SKIN PEPPERS

Chongqing

Hot and Sour No

STICKY GARLIC RIBS WITH FRESH CHILLI AND VINEGAR SAUCE

NYONYA-STYLE SAGO PUDDING

GO

SHRIM

STIR-FRIED LEAFY GREENS

SPECIAL FRIED RICE

NOO

SICHUAN SAUSAGE SANGAS

BLISTERED

steamed savoury egg custard two ways

GREEN BEANS

CHINESE EVERYDAY STOCK

Wonton Noodle Soup